KT-466-605

Windows 8 & RT
for the
Older Generation

Jim Gatenby

BERNARD BABANI (publishing) LTD
The Grampians
Shepherds Bush Road
London W6 7NF
England

www.babanibooks.com

withdrawn from stock

3011780034581 7

Please Note

Although every care has been taken with the production of this book to ensure that all information is correct at the time of writing and that any projects, designs, modifications and/or programs, etc., contained herewith, operate in a correct and safe manner and also that any components specified are normally available in Great Britain, the Publishers and Author do not accept responsibility in any way for the failure (including fault in design) of any project, design, modification or program to work correctly or to cause damage to any equipment that it may be connected to or used in conjunction with, or in respect of any other damage or injury that may be so caused, nor do the Publishers accept responsibility in any way for the failure to obtain specified components.

Notice is also given that if equipment that is still under warranty is modified in any way or used or connected with home-built equipment then that warranty may be void.

© 2013 BERNARD BABANI (publishing) LTD

First Published – February 2013

British Library Cataloguing in Publication Data:

A catalogue record for this book is available from the British Library

ISBN 978-0-85934-739-6

Cover Design by Gregor Arthur

Printed and bound in Great Britain for Bernard Babani (publishing) Ltd

Preface

Windows 8 is the latest version of the Windows operating system used on most laptop and desktop computers. Windows RT is a special version of Windows 8 designed for certain types of tablet computer. From the user's point of view both Windows 8 and Windows RT are almost identical; the differences which do exist are discussed in Chapter 9. The most innovative feature is the new *Start Screen*, consisting of a matrix of colourful tiles. Each tile is a clearly labelled link to a program or *app*. Some tiles include images and others show live information such as regularly changing news headlines and *notifications*. Windows 8 and RT both come with a large number of apps already installed and thousands more can be downloaded from the Windows Store, many of them for free.

This book is intended to help you get to grips with Windows 8 or RT, whether using a brand new computer or upgrading an existing one. (Windows RT cannot be used for upgrades). The first chapter gives an overview of the new operating systems and some of the pre-installed apps. Next the new Start Screen and *Modern User Interface* and their use with either a touch screen or a mouse and keyboard are described. The book then shows how to set up the computer to match your personal preferences for screen designs and colours, etc., followed by Ease of Access features to help with any special needs.

The setting up of an Internet connection is described as is connecting to a printer, followed by Internet security precautions. Finding information, communicating with others using e-mail and social networking are then explained. The use of Skype to make free worldwide telephone calls is also described. The final chapter explains how consumers can obtain Windows 8 and Windows RT and also discusses issues of compatibility.

This book is by the same author as the best-selling and highly acclaimed "Basic Computing for the Older Generation" (ISBN 9780859347310).

About the Author

Jim Gatenby trained as a Chartered Mechanical Engineer and initially worked at Rolls-Royce Ltd using computers in the analysis of jet engine performance. He obtained a Master of Philosophy degree in Mathematical Education by research at Loughborough University of Technology and taught mathematics and computing in school for many years before becoming a full-time author. His most recent teaching posts included Head of Computer Studies. The author has written many books in the fields of educational computing and Microsoft Windows, including many of the titles in the highly successful "Older Generation" series from Bernard Babani (publishing) Ltd.

The author has considerable experience of teaching students of all ages and abilities, in school and in adult education. For several years he successfully taught the well-established CLAIT course and also GCSE Computing and Information Technology.

Trademarks

Microsoft, Windows, Windows XP, Windows Vista, Windows 7, Windows 8, Windows 8 Pro, Windows RT, Surface, Surface Pro, Windows Live Mail, Office, Word, Excel, PowerPoint, OneNote, Paint, Skype and Publisher are either trademarks or registered trademarks of Microsoft Corporation. Facebook is a registered trademark of Facebook, Inc. Twitter is a registered trademark of Twitter, Inc. BT is a registered trademark of British Telecommunications plc. Google is a registered trademark of Google, Inc. All other brand and product names used in this book are recognized as trademarks or registered trademarks, of their respective companies.

Acknowledgements

I would like to thank my wife Jill and our son David for their help and support during the preparation of this book. Also Michael Babani for making this project possible.

Contents

3

Personalizing Windows 8   29

7

Electronic Mail   **79**

8

Social Networking   **91**

9

Why Change to Windows 8 or Windows RT?

Earlier versions of Windows such as Windows XP and Windows 7 are still very popular. This raises the question "why bother to change to Windows 8 or RT?" I have been an enthusiastic user of Windows XP and Windows 7 from their beginnings. However, in recent months I have used both Windows 8 and Windows RT on tablet, laptop and desktop computers and believe they have the following advantages:

- The new Start Screen and its clearly labelled tiles are more explicit than the traditional Windows icons.

- The tiles make it easier to locate and launch programs (or *apps* in the latest jargon).

- *Live* tiles also keep you informed of the latest news and *notifications* inform you of new e-mails, etc.

- Windows 8 and RT start up faster than earlier versions of Windows. Programs also appear to run faster.

- Thousands of apps for (it seems) every conceivable purpose are available to be downloaded from the Windows Store. Many of these are free.

- Programs such as Internet Explorer 10 occupy the whole of the screen, with toolbars hidden in the background but viewable when required.

- You don't need a more powerful computer — an older machine can be upgraded using Windows 8 Pro.

- Windows 8 and Windows 8 Pro can run traditional Windows software.

- Windows RT includes its own versions of the world-beating Office 2013 software including Word and Excel.

It's well worth the effort to acquire the skills needed to use Windows 8 and RT. The Modern User Interface represents the future, being used on all types of computer from touchscreen tablets and smartphones to laptop and desktop machines.

Introducing Windows 8 & RT

What is Windows?

Stored inside every computer there is a suite of software known as the *operating system*. This manages and controls every aspect of the computer's operation, no matter what *application* or *app* (such as a Web browser, music or photo editing program) you are running. The operating system provides the *Start Screen* (or *Desktop*) with *tiles*, *icons* and other screen objects used to launch programs. Recently the explosion in the use of *tablet* computers has seen a corresponding increase in the use of *touchscreens* as a method of input.

The operating system used in over 90% of the world's computers is called *Microsoft Windows*. The latest version, Windows 8, can be used with the new breed of touchscreen tablets, as well as desktop and laptop computers which use a mouse and keyboard. Shown below is the Windows 8 Start Screen, based on *tiles* which are tapped with a finger or clicked with a mouse to launch programs or apps. Some tiles display live information such as news, weather and sport which is regularly updated.

The Modern User Interface

The user interface refers to the way humans interact with the computer. In the last few years this has generally been with a keyboard and mouse (or a touchpad on a laptop). Before that programs and data were launched and run using just a keyboard. (Some of us are old enough to remember entering programs (now called apps) on a deck of punched cards.)

When Microsoft first announced Windows 8 with its radically different user interface, the design was initially called *Metro*. At the time of writing the new interface is called the *Modern UI*.

At the centre of the Modern UI is the Start Screen shown on page 1. There are several editions of Windows 8 but all of them use the same Start Screen, with a common core of default tiles. As you add new apps yourself they are given new tiles and you may have to scroll the Start Screen to see them all. The Start Screen is used to launch programs and this can be done in two ways:

- On a computer with a touchscreen, tap the tile for the app with your finger.

- On a laptop or desktop computer which doesn't have a touchscreen, click the tile with the mouse left button.

The Windows Desktop

Earlier versions of the Windows operating system, such as Windows XP, Vista and Windows 7 have a user interface known as the Windows Desktop. This was designed to be used with a mouse and keyboard. Programs are mainly launched on the Desktop by clicking them on a pop-up Start menu on the left-hand side of the screen or by double-clicking icons on the Desktop. Programs currently running or frequently used appear on a Taskbar across the bottom of the screen, as shown below.

All editions of the new Windows 8 operating system give access to a modified Desktop, as shown below.

The Desktop in Windows 8 is similar to the Desktop in Windows 7, for example, but does not have the Windows 7 Start menu. The Desktop in Windows 8 is used to run programs which were designed for earlier versions of Windows. These programs appear as apps on the Start Screen, alongside of apps specifically designed for the Modern UI. When you tap or click the tile for a program designed for an earlier version of Windows, the program is launched in the Windows 8 Desktop.

There is a tile for the Desktop on the Start Screen, (displaying tulips) shown above and on the left below, which takes you straight to the Windows 8 Desktop. You can switch from the Windows 8 Desktop back to the Modern UI Start Screen in several different ways, as discussed in Chapter 2. One very simple way (if you are using a suitable keyboard) is to press the Windows Logo key, as shown on the right.

Windows 8 & Windows 8 Pro

The basic edition Windows 8 and its close relation Windows 8 Pro can run on a laptop, desktop or tablet computer that can use Windows XP and Windows 7 for example. Windows 8 is intended to be installed by the manufacturers of new computers. Windows 8 Pro is intended for consumers to purchase to upgrade a computer currently using an earlier version of Windows.

Windows 8 and Windows 8 Pro can be used on any laptop, desktop or tablet computer having the common PC architecture known as *x86*. This means computers using processors made by Intel or AMD for example. These have been at the heart of most PC-type computers for many years.

Windows RT

This is a special version of Windows 8 and has been designed for tablet computers which use the *ARM* processor. The ARM is a very popular processor used in many tablets and smartphones because it has a low power consumption. Windows RT cannot generally run traditional Windows software, but relies on new *apps* written specially for it and obtainable from the *Windows Store* as discussed later in this book.

Windows RT is not available to buy separately — it is only available preinstalled on a new tablet computer which uses the ARM processor, such as the Microsoft Surface shown on the next page.

The Microsoft Surface tablet is designed to be used in touchscreen mode. However, there is also a cover which contains an integral keyboard and touchpad. Windows RT includes special versions of Microsoft's widely used Office 2013 suite of software, i.e. Word, Excel, PowerPoint and OneNote.

The Surface can be used both as a tablet, e.g. while on the move, etc. It can also be used for more demanding work by using the integral keyboard cover. As it has a USB port you can also attach a full-size USB keyboard and mouse.

The Microsoft Surface shown above is supplied with Windows RT already installed. The Surface Pro is a more expensive version of the Surface tablet, based on the x86 processor and designed to run Windows 8 Pro.

Windows 8, Windows 8 Pro and Windows RT are all suitable for the home user. Windows Pro is the same as the basic Windows 8 but contains additional features for the professional or advanced user, such as extra security.

Please Note:

- Chapters 1-8 in this book apply to Windows RT and to Windows 8 and Windows 8 Pro. As far as the user is concerned, all three versions of the new Windows operating system look identical and are operated in exactly the same way.

- In general, unless otherwise stated, the term Windows 8 applies to Windows 8, Windows 8 Pro and Windows RT.

- The main differences which do exist between the above versions of Windows are described in detail in Chapter 9.

Key Points: Windows RT and Windows 8

Windows RT

- To obtain Windows RT you must buy a tablet computer with an ARM processor and Windows RT preinstalled.

- Windows RT will not generally run software written for earlier versions of Windows such as Windows 7. Some Windows software such as Office 2013 has been specially converted to run on Windows RT.

- You cannot upgrade an older x86 machine to run Windows RT, or buy separate retail versions of the RT software.

Windows 8 & Windows 8 Pro

- You can upgrade a x86 laptop, desktop or tablet computer to Windows 8 from an earlier version of Windows such as Windows XP, Vista or Windows 7.

- You can buy a new x86 laptop or desktop or tablet computer with Windows 8 (but not RT) already installed. This should run software designed for earlier versions of Windows, such as Windows XP and Windows 7.

Please Note:

- Windows RT and Windows 8 can be operated either with a touchscreen or by using a mouse/touchpad and keyboard.

- Touchscreen tablet computers like the Microsoft Surface may also have an optional keyboard and touchpad.

- Some tablets, such as the Surface, have either a USB port or a *docking station*, enabling a full-size USB keyboard and mouse to be connected for more demanding work.

- Most laptop and desktop computers do not generally support touchscreen operation unless fitted with a special touchscreen monitor.

The Start Screen in Detail

This is the most striking change between Windows 8 and earlier versions such as Windows XP and Windows 7. On starting up the familiar Desktop is replaced by a new Start Screen. Gone are the previous Start Menu and Taskbar to be replaced by a matrix of square and rectangular tiles, shown in the sample below.

Tiles on the Start Screen

Some tiles behave in a similar way to Desktop icons. For example, the tile shown on the right is used to open a new version of the Microsoft Web browser, Internet Explorer 10. The program is launched by tapping with a finger or clicking with a mouse. Internet Explorer 10 is included with Windows 8 and the tile shown on the right above appears on the Start Screen by default.

When you install additional apps, tiles for them may be automatically created on the Start Screen. The tile on the right appeared after the Adobe Reader software was installed. Adobe Reader is used to read documents in the Portable Document Format (PDF), widely used on the Internet.

Live Tiles

Some tiles, such as **News**, **Sport**, **Weather** and **Finance** display constantly changing headlines and live information. A sample headline on the **Finance** tile is shown on the right. After a few seconds the headlines in the **Finance** tile change, to display the FTSE index, as shown below right. Tapping or clicking the **Finance** tile leads to a full screen of news reports, as shown in the example below. To scroll through the news items, swipe across the screen or use a mouse to drag the horizontal scroll bar, as shown at the bottom of the screenshot below.

As discussed in Chapter 2, there are several ways to return to the Start Screen at any time or to launch new apps. You can have several apps running in the background at the same time and cycle through them, before switching to a different app on the screen. You can easily close running apps but this is not essential as they are closed when the computer is shut down.

The Travel App

When you tap or click the **Travel** tile, you can choose from an array of small images of the world's major cities. The **Destinations** feature shows full screen photos such as **Venice** below and you can also see 360 degree panoramic views of major attractions.

The **Travel** app also lists hotels, restaurants and tourist information, as shown below.

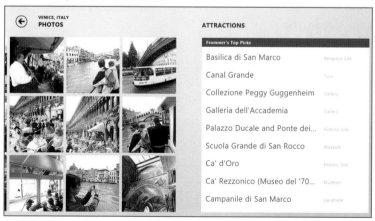

The Mail App

Many of the apps which appear as tiles on the Start Screen are discussed in more detail later in this book. The **Mail** tile leads to a new, fully featured e-mail program as shown below. E-mail is discussed in more detail in Chapter 7.

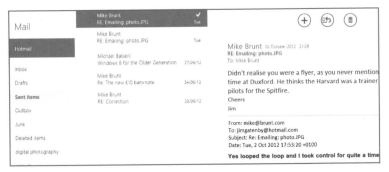

The People App

This helps you to keep in touch with friends on social networking sites such as Facebook and Twitter. Social networking is discussed in detail in Chapter 8.

The Weather App

This allows you to find out 10-day weather forecasts for any selected location, both where you live or worldwide.

The Photos App

This gives access to all of your photos stored in various locations such as the Pictures Library on your computer, on the Internet in the SkyDrive "Clouds", or on the Facebook  or Flickr Web sites. The Photos tile is live, presenting a regularly changing mini slideshow of photos.

The Maps App

This presents a map of the world but also allows you to zoom in on a particular area such as your own location. Zooming in and out is achieved with the pinching and stretching gestures with two fingers on a touch screen or by holding down the **Ctrl** key and using the central scroll wheel on a mouse. Maps can be displayed in Road view, as shown below or in Aerial view.

The SkyDrive App

SkyDrive is a storage facility on the Internet where you can place copies of your documents and photos, etc. This means they can be shared with friends, family or colleagues anywhere in the world. All they need is an Internet connection and a Web browser on any device such as a smartphone, tablet computer, laptop or  desktop machine. This form of remote storage of documents and photos, etc., away from your own computer is referred to as *cloud computing*. SkyDrive is also discussed in Chapter 7.

Viewing All of Your Apps

All of the apps or programs installed on your computer can be displayed using the **All apps** icon shown on the right. To display the icon on a touchscreen, from the Start Screen shown on page 1, swipe in from the top or bottom edge.

Alternatively right click over the Start Screen to display the **All apps** icon. Tap or click the icon to reveal all of the apps. Flick the screen with a finger or drag the horizontal scroll bar at the bottom of the screen if necessary, to reveal another part of the screen.

Many of the apps are included with Windows 8 itself, while others can be downloaded from the *Windows Store* as discussed in Chapter 6.

The *Windows Explorer* used in previous versions of Windows is still present in *Windows 8*, though in Windows RT it is known as the *File Explorer*. This is used to manage all of your documents and other files in a hierarchical system of folders. As mentioned earlier, apps need to be specially written or converted for the Windows RT tablet with its ARM processor.

Also present in Windows 8 are the graphics program *Windows Paint* and the *Control Panel (*shown below), used to manage the computer and the settings for various devices.

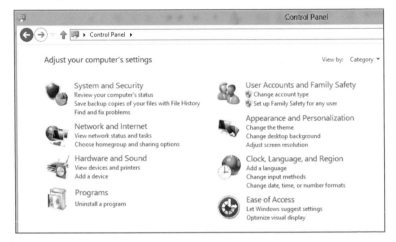

Obtaining More Apps from the Windows Store

This allows users of all versions of Windows 8 to download and install on their computers both free and paid for apps in a wide range of subjects, such as games, music and video and photography. The Windows Store is discussed in Chapter 6.

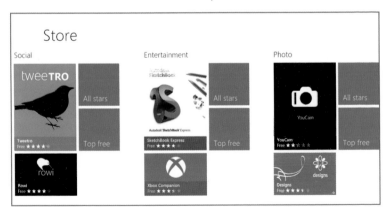

Navigating Windows 8

Introduction

You can use all editions of Windows 8 (including Windows RT) with a touchscreen or with a mouse and keyboard. Users of tablet computers may be able to choose between these two modes of operation, while many desktop and laptop computers can only be controlled by a mouse and keyboard. To use touch operation with a laptop or desktop computer, a special touch-sensitive screen is required.

When you switch the computer on, it quickly boots, i.e. starts up, to display the Lock Screen, shown below. (Alternative Lock Screen designs can be selected, as discussed in Chapter 3). Either swipe your finger diagonally across a touchscreen or click anywhere on the screen using a mouse. Then enter the password for your Microsoft account. This is set up during the sign-up process when Windows 8 is first installed.

The next two pages list some common Windows 8 mouse operations and the corresponding touchscreen *gestures*.

Basic Mouse Operations

Click

Press the left mouse button to select an object on the screen at the current cursor position, such as a menu option. Opens an app from its tile on the Start Screen.

Double-click

Two left clicks in quick succession to open a folder in the Windows (or File) Explorer. Also launches an app from an icon.

Right-click

Press the right mouse button to open a shortcut or context sensitive menu. These menus list options relevant to the current cursor position.

Drag

Click over a screen object, then keeping the left button held down drag the object to a new position, before releasing the left button. Can be used to change the position of a tile on the Start Screen or move a file or folder to a different folder in the Windows Explorer (or File Explorer in Windows RT). Drag is also used to move horizontal or vertical scroll bars to advance forwards or backwards through a long document. Dragging an object to another disc drive, *copies* the object. Dragging an object to a new location on the same disc drive *moves* the object. Dragging with the right button held down displays a menu when the button is released. This includes options to move or copy the item.

Scroll Wheel

This wheel in the centre of a mouse is used to scroll through a long document on the screen.

Ctrl + Scroll Wheel

Hold down the Ctrl key and turn the scroll wheel. This zooms in or out of whatever is currently displayed on the screen.

Basic Touch Gestures

Tap

Press quickly but gently on the screen to launch an app from a tile on the Start Screen, or select an option from a menu.

Double Tap

Two quick taps to open a folder or flash drive, etc., in Windows/File Explorer. To find out about devices such as a printer, double tap its icon in Devices and Printers in the Control Panel.

Tap and Hold

Keep your finger gently pressing against an object or area of the screen for a few seconds then release to display a shortcut menu relevant to the current screen location.

Drag

Keeping your finger over a screen object such as a tile on the Start Screen or a file in Windows/File Explorer, move your finger over the screen and release to drop the object in its new location.

Swipe

This involves sliding your finger across the screen, usually from one of the four edges. Swiping has many uses for displaying running apps and options and these are discussed in detail shortly.

Flick

The finger is quickly moved across the screen horizontally or vertically to scroll through a long document.

Rotate two fingers to turn an object.

Pinch or move two fingers together to zoom out.

Stretch or move two fingers apart to zoom in or enlarge.

The *bezel* or border around a tablet screen is touch sensitive. When you swipe from the left, right, top or bottom edge of the screen, always start with your finger in the bezel area.

Launching Apps Using Tiles

After you enter your password, the Start Screen appears as shown below. The background colour can be changed if you wish, as discussed in Chapter 3.

If you want to change the position of a particular app it can be dragged and dropped to a new position, as mentioned on the previous pages.

To launch a particular app, such as Internet Explorer, tap or click its tile, as shown on the right and above.

Near the top of the screenshot at the bottom of the previous page there is the **Bing** search bar. Here you can enter keywords to find information about topics which interest you, such as **Magna Carta** for example. At the bottom of the Internet Explorer window on the previous page is an Address Bar, which by default displays **http://www.bing.com** as shown below.

Type the address of a Web site here, replacing **www.bing.com**, and press the Enter or Return key to launch the Web site.

Returning to the Start Screen from an App

There are several ways to return to the Start Screen at any time. With the Surface tablet there is a Start button on the bottom bezel or edge of the screen. A Start *Charm* also appears on the Charms Bar when you swipe in from the right-hand edge, as discussed on page 23. With a mouse, hover the cursor in the top or bottom right-hand corner of the screen to see the Start Charm.

Alternatively swipe in and back again (a few centimetres) from the left-hand side of a touchscreen screen without lifting your finger off. A thumbnail image of the Start Screen appears in the bottom left-hand corner of the screen, as shown on the right. This thumbnail also appears if you hover a mouse cursor over the bottom left-hand corner of the screen. Tap or click the thumbnail to open the Start Screen full-size as shown at the top of page 18.

If you are using a full keyboard it may have a Windows Logo key like the one shown on the right. This allows you to switch between the Start Screen and the app, i.e. program, you are currently running.

Launching an App by Typing its Name

If you are using a keyboard and can't see the tile for an App on the Start Screen, a quick way to launch an App is to begin typing its name while the Start Screen is displayed on the screen. For example, to launch the **Weather** app, as soon as you type **W** a list of the apps beginning with that letter are displayed.

However, as soon as "**We**" is entered only the **Weather** app is listed, as shown below.

Tap or click inside the small rectangle containing the word **Weather** on the left above, to launch the application.

With a touchscreen, select the Start Screen and swipe inwards from the top or bottom edge. The **All apps** icon appears, as shown on the right. Tap the **All apps** icon to view all of the apps on the computer and then tap the appropriate tile to launch the app you require.

Switching Apps

You can have lots of apps running in the background at the same time. To cycle through the apps that are currently running, swipe in from the left-hand edge, starting from the bezel. With a mouse, keep clicking in the top left-hand corner. The apps are displayed one at a time on the full screen. Stop at the app you want to use.

Swipe in a few centimetres from the left-hand edge and back again to see thumbnails of all the apps currently running, as shown down the left-hand edge below. Or hover the cursor over the top or bottom left corner then move the cursor up or down the left edge of the screen. Alternatively hold down the Windows Logo key and press the Tab key. Tap or click on a thumbnail as shown down the left-hand side below to switch to the new app.

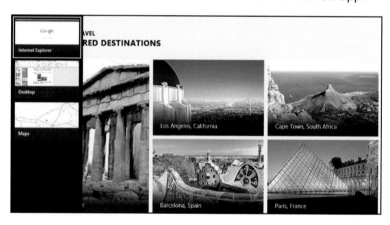

Holding down Alt and pressing Tab displays all the running apps as thumbnails across the centre of the screen, as shown below. Stop pressing Tab and release the Alt key when you have highlighted the app you want to run on the full screen.

Multi-tasking: Displaying Two Apps Side by Side

Normally one app fills the whole screen while several others may be running in the background. However, you can have two apps running side by side in separate windows. Swipe an app about six centimetres in from the left edge and briefly hold until the app fills the left panel as shown below. Alternatively with a mouse drag the top of the app downwards and to the left or the right. The app then appears in a narrow window on the left or right of the screen, with a vertical line separating the apps.

To change the app in a panel, swipe a new app in from the left-hand edge. Stop in either the left or right panel and the new app will open to fill that panel. When you open a new app from the Start Screen by clicking with a mouse, it fills the larger screen.

To close the split screen, place your finger or cursor over the dividing line then drag to the left-hand edge of the screen.

Closing an App

An app can be closed by swiping down the app from the top edge of the screen. Alternatively with a mouse, drag the top edge of the app down the screen. The app shrinks and can be dragged and dropped completely off the bottom of the screen.

The Charms Bar

Swipe in from the right-hand edge of the screen to reveal the Charms Bar shown here below on the left. Alternatively use a mouse to hover the cursor in either the bottom right-hand corner or the top right-hand corner of the screen. The charms are transparent at first but appear as shown below on the left after you move the cursor upwards or downwards through the charms. The touch cover keyboard on the Surface tablet has keys for each of the charms. Alternatively hold down the Windows Logo key and press **C**.

The top charm, **Search** can scan many categories of information stored on your computer or on the Internet. Searching for an **App** was discussed on page 20. There are many other categories to search through, such as **Settings**, **Files**, **Finance** and **Internet Explorer** as shown below.

In the example below, with **News** selected, the keywords **Gas prices** were entered into the Search bar. When you   tap or click the magnifying glass search icon, the screen displays a large selection of

headlines and extracts from news agencies and newspapers, as shown below. Some of these stories are very new, perhaps posted in the last hour, for example. Drag or scroll to see all of the headlines and abstracts.

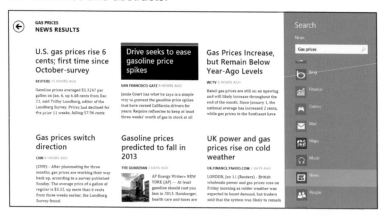

Tap or click a headline, etc., to read the full article.

The **Share** option on the Charms Bar on page 23 allows you to share information or photos, etc., with other people.

Start returns you to the Start Screen. If you're already on the Start Screen, the computer switches to the most recent app.

Devices on the Charms Bar lists any printers, speakers, etc., connected to the computer or on a home network. These only appear when you are using an app with something to print, such as the **Mail** app.

The Settings Charm

The **Settings** charm shown below on the right and on the Charms Bar on page 23 leads to some of the most important settings on your computer.

When you select the **Settings** charm shown on the right, the icons shown below appear at the bottom right of the screen. These give information about your Internet connection, (e.g. **BTHomeHub...**) and your sound and brightness settings, for example.

Change PC settings shown on the bottom right below leads to a list called **PC settings** as shown on the next page.

Personalize shown below provides different colour schemes and designs for your screens. **Ease of Access** at the bottom of the screenshot below allows you to make adjustments and select features designed to help with special needs.

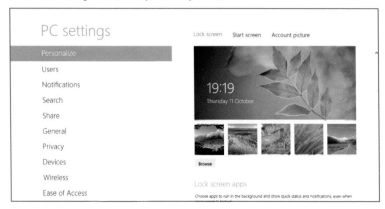

Important settings and personalizing the computer are discussed in more detail in the next chapter.

Shutting Down the Computer

At the end of a computing session always shut down correctly. Otherwise you might damage any files that are open. Select the **Settings** charm as discussed on the previous page and tap or click the **Power** icon shown on the right above and in context below. Then tap or click **Shut down** or **Update and shut down** from the small menu which pops up, as shown on the right above. This closes all apps that are currently running and switches off the computer.

Sleep Mode

Selecting **Sleep** on the small **Power** menu at the bottom of the previous page puts the computer in a low power consumption mode. This saves electricity while you are not using the computer. Your work and settings are saved and to resume work later press the power button on your computer.

Your computer will enter Sleep mode automatically if it is not used for a period of time. The period of time can be set in the computer's Control Panel as shown below. The Control Panel is a feature of Windows used to alter many important settings as discussed later in this book.

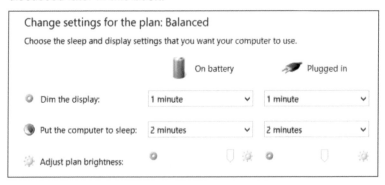

Tap or click the arrow on the right of **2 minutes** shown above to display a menu of optional time periods, ranging from 1 minute to 5 hours before Sleep mode is launched. There is also a **Never** option. Select the required time and tap or click **Save changes**.

Sleep mode is useful if you want to leave your computer for a while and the screen is displaying confidential information. When you return, press the power button and the computer will resume where you left off with the same files, documents and apps running. The Control Panel can be used to set the Lock Screen (shown on page 15) to appear when the power button on the computer is pressed. Tap or click anywhere on the Lock Screen, then enter your password to resume your previous activities.

Keyboard Shortcuts

If you use a keyboard like the one below with keys such as **Ctrl**, **Alt**, **Tab** and the Windows Logo key, shown on the right, you may find the following key presses useful as alternatives to the touchscreen or mouse, etc.

Keyboard Shortcuts

Alt+F4   Close the current app.

Alt+Tab   Cycle through all open Desktop and Modern UI apps displayed horizontally across the screen.

F1   Help.

Win   Alternate between current app and the Start Screen.

Win+C   Display the Charms Bar.

Win+F   Search files.

Win+X   Display shortcuts menu.

Win+Tab   Display open Modern UI apps as thumbnails down the left of the screen.

Example:

Alt+F4 means: "While holding down the **Alt** key, press the **F4** key".

Personalizing Windows 8

Introduction

Windows 8 provides a number of ways for you to customise the computer to suit your own particular needs and preferences. These include:

- Selecting a different background design for the Lock Screen. This appears when you first start the computer or if you wake it up from sleep mode.

- Changing the colour scheme for the Start Screen. This is the main screen used to launch apps, shown on page 1.

- Creating or changing your account picture used to identify you, e.g. by including it in the e-mails you send.

- Selecting a different background design for the Windows Desktop discussed on pages 2 and 3.

- Changing the colour scheme for the windows borders and the Taskbar along the bottom of the Desktop.

- Changing the *screen resolution*. This is the number of *pixels* or picture elements in the horizontal and vertical directions. Windows 8 requires a minimum resolution of 1024x768 pixels, with more needed for some tasks.

- Using the Ease of Access Center, which provides features to help anyone with special needs, such as the magnifier to enlarge text and the on-screen keyboard for anyone struggling to use a physical keyboard.

The Lock Screen

This is the screen which appears when the computer starts up or when you wake it from sleep. Open the Charms bar as described on page 23 and from the **Settings** charm, shown on the right, select **Change PC settings**. Then select **Personalize** from the left-hand panel, as shown below. With **Lock screen** selected at the top of the screen you can see the current design in the right-hand panel, while along the bottom there's a choice of different Lock Screens.

Using Your Own Picture for the Lock Screen

If you don't wish to use any of the designs provided, select **Browse** to search the photos and pictures on your computer, etc. Next select with a tick the picture you wish to use and then select **Choose picture**, as shown below.

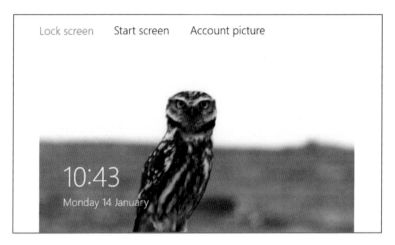

Apart from your chosen picture, as shown above, the Lock Screen also displays the current date and time, *notifications* of new e-mails, remaining battery life and your Internet connection.

The Start Screen

As shown at the top above, there is an option to change the colour scheme for the Start Screen. Tap or click the colours on the bottom horizontal bar or drag the arrow heads to experiment with different colour schemes. The grid of 20 small squares shown below allows you to choose an artistic pattern to superimpose on the main background colour you have chosen.

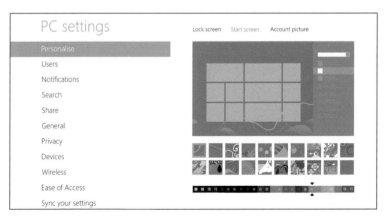

Your Account Picture

You can create or change your account picture after selecting **Account picture**, as shown below on the top right.

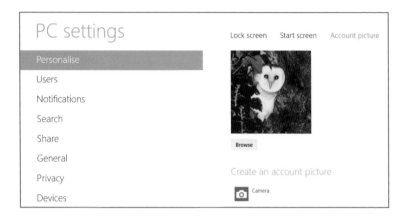

If you have a suitable image stored on your computer's hard disc or on a removable disc or flash drive, select **Browse**, as shown above under the picture, to search for and insert the image. Select with a tick the image you wish to use then select **Choose image**.

Alternatively if you have a tablet or laptop computer with a built-in camera or a desktop machine with a plug-in webcam, tap or click the camera icon shown on the right and above to create a new account photo.

Your account picture appears in several places, such as the Welcome screen as the computer starts up, on the right-hand side of the Start Screen, as shown on the right and on the top of any e-mails you send using the Windows 8 Mail app.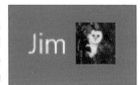

Locking the Screen

If you tap or click your account picture on the Start Screen, a small menu pops up as shown below.

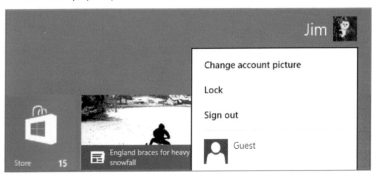

Change account picture shown above opens the PC settings window shown on the previous page. **Account picture** is already selected and the picture can be changed after selecting **Browse** as described on the previous page.

If you select **Lock** shown above, the Lock Screen is displayed. The computer can now only be used by someone who knows the password. This is entered after swiping upwards from the bottom of a touchscreen or with a mouse, clicking anywhere on the screen.

Sign out shown in the top screenshot also returns you to the Lock Screen shown on the right above and requires a new user to sign in as shown on the right.

Changing the Windows Desktop Background

The Desktop will probably be used a lot on your computer so you may wish to give it your own personal touch. First open the Control Panel. With a touch screen, swipe in from the bottom of the Start Screen, select the **All apps** icon which appears and then scroll across and select **Control Panel** from the large array of apps which fills the screen.

To open the Control Panel when using a keyboard and mouse, from the Start Screen, start typing "**con...**", etc. and then select **Control Panel**

when it appears on the screen, as shown above. Under **Appearance and Personalization**, select **Change desktop background**. Windows provides several designs for the Desktop background. If you select more than one, the background takes the form of a slide show.

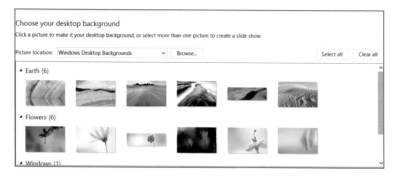

Quick Ways to Open the Control Panel Using a Mouse

Right-click in the extreme bottom left-hand corner of the screen and then select **Control Panel** from the shortcut pop-up menu as shown on page 45. Alternatively right-click over **Control Panel** in **All apps** as discussed earlier and select **Pin to Start**. This places a tile for the Control Panel on the Start Screen.

Using Your Own Photos as the Desktop Background

If you have photos of your own, these can be used as the desktop background. In the screenshot below, the **Browse** button was selected from above the right-hand image, then **Computer** was selected from the pop-up **Browse For Folder** window. (The Computer feature displays a list of all of your hard discs and removable discs). After selecting the hard disc **(C:)** the folder **Harness Racing** was selected as shown below and opened by tapping (or clicking) **OK**.

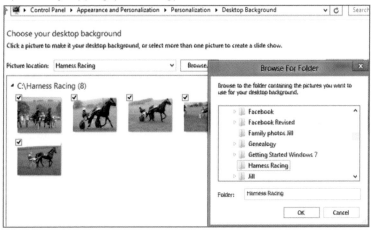

All of the required photos were selected with a tick in the top left-hand corner as shown above. After selecting **Save changes** a slide show of the photos is placed on the Windows Desktop.

Changing the Windows Border Colours

This includes the colour of the Taskbar along the bottom of the Windows Desktop. Open the Control Panel as described on the previous page. Select the green heading **Appearance and Personalization** and then under **Personalization** select **Change the colour of your taskbar and window borders**.

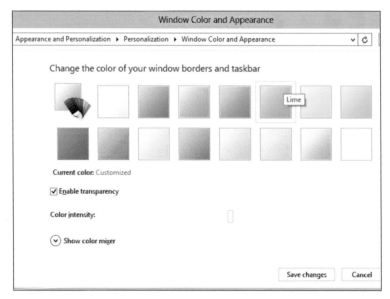

Before finally selecting a colour for your windows' borders and the Taskbar along the bottom of the Desktop, you may wish to experiment with **transparency**, **Color intensity** and the **color mixer**, as shown above. Then select **Save changes** to put the new settings into effect. In the example below, the colour **Twilight** was chosen for the border and the Taskbar, with transparency disabled and the intensity set at high.

Changing the Size of Text and Icons, etc.

If you're finding the text and other items difficult to see on the screen, there are ways of enlarging them. From the **Control Panel** select **Appearance and Personalization**, followed by **Display** and then **Make text and other items larger or smaller**.

Display
Make text and other items larger or smaller   Adjust screen resolution

The **Display** window opens, as shown below. To change the size of all of the objects on the screen including icons, images and text, select **Custom sizing options**. Then either select a different percentage or drag the ruler which appears. To change only the size of the text in windows, for example in the title bars or in menu options, use the drop-down menu under **Change the text size only**. As discussed shortly, the **Magnifier** allows you to enlarge a small selected area of the screen.

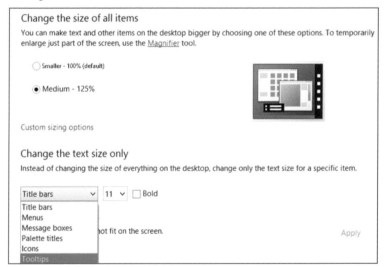

Change the size of all items

You can make text and other items on the desktop bigger by choosing one of these options. To temporarily enlarge just part of the screen, use the Magnifier tool.

○ Smaller - 100% (default)

◉ Medium - 125%

Custom sizing options

Change the text size only

Instead of changing the size of everything on the desktop, change only the text size for a specific item.

| Title bars | ∨ | 11 ∨ | ☐ Bold |

Title bars
Menus
Message boxes   not fit on the screen.   Apply
Palette titles
Icons
Tooltips

The text on a tablet or touchscreen may be enlarged or made smaller using two-fingered stretching or pinching gestures.

Changing the Screen Resolution

A *pixel* (picture element) is a single point in a screen display. The screen resolution is usually quoted in the format 1024x768, representing the number of pixels in the horizontal and vertical directions respectively. 1024x768 is stated as the minimum resolution for Windows 8 with 1366x768 recommended for some applications. At the higher resolutions, objects appear sharper and smaller. The maximum resolution available depends on the specification of the monitor and the graphics components in the computer which control the screen display.

To check the resolution on your computer, from the **Appearance and Personalization** section in the **Control Panel**, as discussed earlier, select **Display** and **Adjust screen resolution**, as shown at the top of the previous page. To change the setting, tap or click the small arrow to the right of the current **Resolution** setting and drag the slider. Then select **Apply** at the bottom right of the Screen Resolution window and either **Keep changes** or **Revert**.

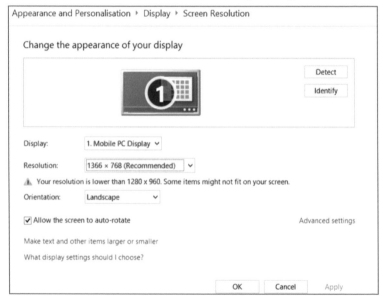

Ease of Access

This chapter describes features in Windows which are designed to help people with special needs, such as impaired eyesight, defective hearing or reduced manual dexterity.

The Magnifier

This makes the screen easier to read by enlarging the entire screen area or just selected parts.

The On-Screen Keyboard

This is intended for anyone who finds the normal physical keyboard difficult to use.

The Narrator

This reads aloud the text on the screen including the title bars and text in Windows as well as documents you're working on.

High Contrast

The screen display is converted to very clear white text on a black background.

Speech Recognition

You control the computer and input data entirely by speaking.

These features are discussed in more detail shortly. You can launch some of the features quickly after selecting the **Settings** charm, then **Change PC settings** and **Ease of Access** as shown on pages 30 and 44. More settings for the Ease of Access features are found in the Control Panel. Open the Control Panel as described on page 34. At the bottom right of the Control Panel there are links to the **Ease of Access** features, as shown below.

Programs
Uninstall a program

Ease of Access
Let Windows suggest settings
Optimise visual display

If you select **Let Windows suggest settings**, shown at the bottom of the previous page, you are presented with a series of statements about any limitations you might have, such as defective eyesight, hearing or manual dexterity.

Eyesight (1 of 5)

Select all statements that apply to you:

☑ Images and text on TV are difficult to see (even when I'm wearing glasses).

☐ Lighting conditions make it difficult to see images on my monitor.

☐ I am blind.

☐ I have another type of vision impairment (even if glasses correct it).

After completing the on-screen statements, Windows recommends a series of settings based on the ticks you have placed in the check boxes, covering the whole range of common impairments. You can accept or reject these settings.

Alternatively select **Ease of Access** as shown at the bottom of page 39, then select **Ease of Access Center**, as shown below.

Ease of Access Center

Let Windows suggest settings   Optimise visual display   Replace sounds with visual cues

Change how your mouse works   Change how your keyboard works

The **Ease of Access Center** is used to start the **Magnifier**, **On-Screen Keyboard**, **Narrator** and **High Contrast** screen.

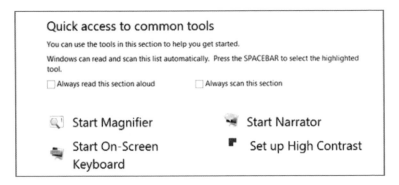

Quick access to common tools

You can use the tools in this section to help you get started.

Windows can read and scan this list automatically. Press the SPACEBAR to select the highlighted tool.

☐ Always read this section aloud   ☐ Always scan this section

Start Magnifier   Start Narrator

Start On-Screen   Set up High Contrast
Keyboard

The Magnifier

Tap or click **Start Magnifier**, as shown on the previous page. The **Magnifier** window opens, initially set at 100% but this can easily be changed using the plus and minus buttons shown below.

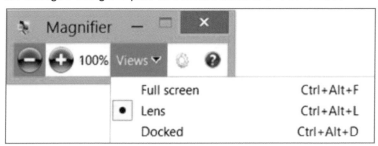

If you tap or click the arrow next to **Views**, shown above, you can choose whether to enlarge the **Full screen** or just the **Lens**. The Lens is a small rectangle which can be dragged around the screen with a finger or mouse, enlarging different areas. The example below uses 200% magnification.

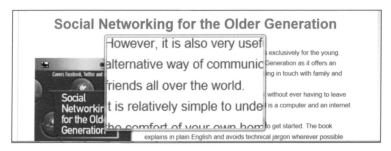

In **Docked** mode a horizontal strip across the top the screen is enlarged. This can be scrolled to display the whole document in large text. After a short time the Magnifier window shown at the top of this page changes to a magnifying glass icon, as shown on the right. This icon can be tapped or clicked to make the Magnifier window reappear on the screen. Tap or click the cross at the top right of the Magnifier window to switch off the Magnifier.

The Narrator

Tap or click **Start Narrator**, as shown at the bottom of page 40. The computer starts to read aloud all of the text on the screen.

You also hear the name of any key you press. The Narrator appears as an icon on the Taskbar on the Desktop as shown on the right and below.

If you tap or click the Narrator icon, the **Narrator Settings** window opens, as shown below. This includes options to alter the speed, pitch and volume of the Narrator voice or to choose a different voice altogether. The Narrator is closed by tapping or clicking the cross in the top right-hand corner of the Narrator Settings window shown below. Alternatively tap or click **Exit** at the bottom of the window.

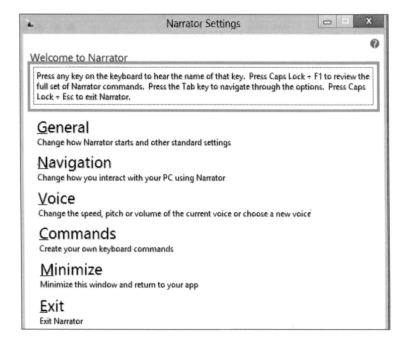

Narrator Settings

Welcome to Narrator

Press any key on the keyboard to hear the name of that key. Press Caps Lock + F1 to review the full set of Narrator commands. Press the Tab key to navigate through the options. Press Caps Lock + Esc to exit Narrator.

General
Change how Narrator starts and other standard settings

Navigation
Change how you interact with your PC using Narrator

Voice
Change the speed, pitch or volume of the current voice or choose a new voice

Commands
Create your own keyboard commands

Minimize
Minimize this window and return to your app

Exit
Exit Narrator

The On-Screen Keyboard

If you have trouble using a physical keyboard, the **On-Screen Keyboard**, shown in Microsoft Word below, may help. This can be operated with a mouse or joystick or another pointing device.

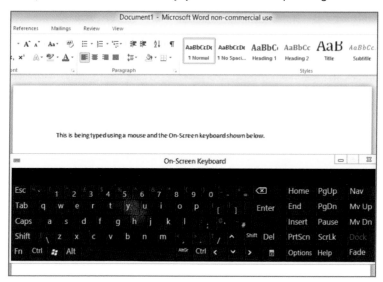

Upper and lower case letters and alternate characters on a key can be obtained by first tapping or clicking either **Caps** or **Shift**. If you have a touchscreen computer such as the Microsoft Surface, you may find it easier to use the larger keys on the virtual keyboard provided as standard with the computer.

High Contrast

Select **Set up High Contrast** as shown on page 40 and then **Choose a High Contrast Theme**. Experiment by selecting and applying different Themes to find one that suits you.

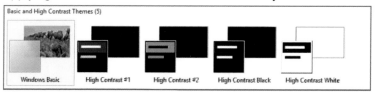

As mentioned earlier, you can quickly open the Ease of Access settings from the Settings charm, as discussed on pages 25 and 26. After selecting **Change PC settings**, select **Ease of Access** under **PC settings** shown highlighted in green below. Tap or click the small rectangles shown below to switch **High Contrast** on or off or make everything on your screen bigger. If you have a computer such as a tablet with a volume control, you can use this to switch the On-Screen Keyboard, the Magnifier or the Narrator on or off. First from the drop-down menu select either **On-Screen Keyboard**, **Magnifier** or **Narrator**. The selected feature can then be switched on or off by holding down the Windows Logo key together with the **Volume Up** control.

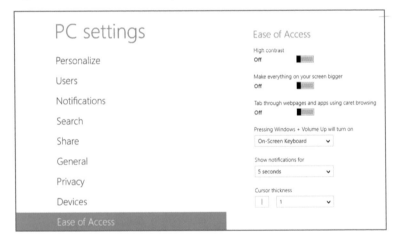

Alternative Methods

In the Windows operating system, there are usually several alternative ways of launching a particular app or feature. The Ease of Access features can be set up for a particular person using the Control Panel, as discussed earlier in this chapter. As shown above, you can also quickly launch the Ease of Access features such as the Magnifier, Narrator, etc., using the PC settings window of the Settings charm, discussed earlier.

Another way to launch the Ease of Access features is from the Apps screen. From the Start Screen, swipe inwards from the top or bottom edge or right-click with a mouse. Then tap or click the **All apps** icon which appears, as shown above on the right. If necessary, scroll across the **All apps** screen until you see the **Ease of Access** features such as the **Magnifier**, etc., as shown on the right. Tap or click to launch the **Magnifier**, **Narrator** or **On-Screen Keyboard**, as discussed earlier in this chapter. **Windows Speech Recognition** is discussed on the next page.

Alternative Ways to Open the Control Panel

As discussed earlier, the Control Panel can be opened by tapping or clicking its name in the All apps feature. Or by typing the first few letters such as "**con"** while the Start Screen is displayed. If you are using a mouse or touchpad, moving the cursor to the bottom left-hand corner of the screen and right-clicking opens the Shortcut Menu as shown on the right. This enables you to launch many important Windows features, such as the **Control Panel**, shown highlighted on the right. Also listed on the right is the **Windows Explorer** which is used to manage all the documents and pictures stored on your computer. In Windows RT the Windows Explorer is known as the File Explorer.

Programs and Features
Mobility Center
Power Options
Event Viewer
System
Device Manager
Disk Management
Computer Management
Command Prompt
Command Prompt (Admin)

Task Manager
Control Panel
Windows Explorer
Search
Run

Desktop

Speech Recognition

This feature allows you to control the computer entirely by spoken commands. The necessary sound facilities are normally built into a tablet or laptop computer but on a desktop machine you may need to add speakers and a microphone. Tasks such as starting programs and opening menus, dictating text and writing and sending e-mails can be achieved without using a touchpad, mouse or keyboard. First you need to learn some spoken commands, by following the Windows Speech Tutorial; you must also "train" the computer to recognise your voice and dialect if you have one.

Tap or click **Speech Recognition** from Ease of Access in the Control Panel, as discussed earlier, as shown below.

Speech Recognition
Start speech recognition   Set up a microphone

The main **Speech Recognition** window is shown below.

Experienced users can click **Start Speech Recognition** or beginners can select **Take Speech Tutorial** as shown above. You can also launch this feature by tapping or clicking **Windows Speech Recognition** on the Apps screen discussed on page 45.

As shown on the previous page, there is a **Set up microphone** option. When you first start Speech Recognition you are given advice on the use of the microphone and you are asked to read a piece of sample text. The Speech Tutorial helps you to practise all of the basic spoken commands such as **Start Listening**, **New Line**, **New Paragraph** and **Correct**. You are given practice at correcting mistakes on the screen and shown how to use voice commands to select menus. Selecting **Train your computer to better understand you** shown on the previous page, launches extensive practice exercises in which you speak into the microphone, while the computer learns to recognise your voice.

After you've finished training yourself (and the computer) you are ready to tap or click **Start Speech Recognition** as shown on the previous page; this displays the microphone user interface shown below:

The user gives voice commands such as **Start listening** to make the computer begin interpreting the commands spoken into the microphone. The microphone button shown on the left above changes colour – blue indicating that the computer is listening to you, grey indicating not listening. The small window in the centre gives text feedback such as **Listening** or **Sleeping**. The message **What was that?** shown in the text window below indicates that a command was not understood by the computer.

If the above message appears you are advised to repeat the command or try a different command.

The Speech Recognition feature allows anyone who can't manipulate a mouse, touchpad or keyboard to use programs such as Microsoft Word, or e-mail, for example. Using only spoken commands, you can create, edit, save and print documents. I have found it quite easy to use the Speech Recognition system to dictate fairly simple documents. Although a microphone headset is recommended, I found the built-in microphones on my Surface tablet and Dell laptop worked well. If necessary, a serviceable plug-in microphone headset for a desktop computer can be bought for a few pounds.

However, it is important to work through the tutorials thoroughly and to spend plenty of time training the computer to recognise your voice. It also helps to speak slowly and clearly into the microphone.

Further Help

In the Control Panel, select **Ease of Access Center** and then **Make touch and tablets easier to use**. The following window opens, including an option for tablet users to choose an accessibility tool (like the Magnifier) to be opened using the Windows Logo button and the Volume Up button on the tablet.

Learn about additional accessibility technologies online at the bottom of the above screenshot is a link to the Microsoft Accessibility Web site. This gives details of products and companies involved in the design of accessibility aids, such as head mounted input devices to overcome physical problems.

5

Getting Connected

Introduction

Whatever type of computer you have — tablet, laptop or desktop machine, the Internet is bound to be a major part of your computing activities. Modern Internet connections use *broadband* technology. This refers to very fast data transfer along special telephone cables. Developments such as fibre optic cables have greatly increased the power of the Internet to download to your computer bulky media such as photographs, music and video. Here are just a few examples:

- Keeping in touch with friends and family anywhere in the world, using e-mail, Skype and social networking websites like Facebook and Twitter. Sharing photos and videos and using live webcams to see people who may be far away.

- Finding the best prices and ordering anything online such as books, holidays and supermarket shopping.

- Buying rail and flight tickets and monitoring actual arrival and departure times in real time.

- Selling surplus goods using the online auction site eBay.

- Searching millions of Web pages to find the latest information on any subject — medical topics, legal advice or hobbies such as gardening or DIY for example.

- Managing your bank accounts and savings online, carrying out major banking transactions. If necessary, filing your Income Tax Self-Assessment online.

- *Downloading* music, videos and apps from the Internet and saving them on your own computer.

Essential Equipment

There are a few things you may need to do before you can start surfing the Internet. It's not difficult and no-one should be put off doing it themselves. The following are the basic requirements:

- A tablet, laptop, or desktop computer with an *Internet adaptor* (or *adapter*) built in or as an add-on accessory.

- An *Internet Access Point* in your home or in a public place such as a hotel or airport.

- An account with an *Internet Service Provider (ISP).*

- A *Web browser* — a computer program or app which is used to navigate and display Web pages.

Internet Adaptor

New tablet and laptop computers have this Internet connectivity built in during manufacture. On a new computer this feature may need to be switched on. Desktop computers generally need a separate Internet adaptor, often in the form of a *dongle* as shown on the right.
The dongle plugs into one of the small rectangular *USB ports* i.e. connecting sockets, on the computer casing.

Internet Access Point

For the home user this normally means a *wireless router* as shown on the right. This is a device which connects to the Internet, usually via a cable which plugs into a telephone socket in your home. Your computer's Internet adaptor transmits and receives data to and from the router using radio waves.

In our house we have a mixture of tablet, laptop and desktop machines scattered about different rooms and sometimes out in the garden. All of them can connect to the Internet via the router, often at the same time.

Wireless networks and technology are often referred to as *WiFi*. Most home networks are now wireless although you can connect a computer to a router using a special *Ethernet* cable. This may be necessary during the initial setting up process.

Network Security

A neighbour with a WiFi computer might detect your network and, without suitable security measures, might access your data. For this reason the router usually has a *password* printed on the back. The password must be entered the first time you go online to the Internet via the router.

Mobile Broadband

Some of the mobile phone networks such as Three and T-Mobile enable you to connect your computer to the Internet using *Mobile Broadband*. So you can go online wherever there is a signal for the mobile phone network. Computers make the connection using a special Mobile Broadband USB dongle instead of the router used on home networks. This dongle is similar in size and appearance to the Internet adaptor shown on the previous page. The mobile broadband dongle contains a SIM card to connect the computer to the Internet. Some tablet computers connect to the Internet using a SIM card inserted directly into a special slot in the tablet's casing.

While mobile broadband is particularly useful for computing on the move using a tablet or laptop computer, a mobile broadband dongle can also be used on a desktop computer in a situation where no broadband telephone landline is available. Many hotels, restaurants, trains and airports provide Internet access points. Some organisations offer a free WiFi connection while others make a charge. In some places you may need to ask for a password to enter before you can go online.

Internet Service Providers (ISPs)

As discussed previously, the main methods of connecting to the Internet are by using a router plugged into the telephone socket in your home or via one of the mobile phone networks. Several ISPs provide a broadband service over the BT telephone landlines including BT themselves. You need to go online and look at the various offers before signing up for a contract. If you don't yet have Internet access perhaps you can get help from a friend or relative. Alternatively use a computer in your local library and do a search for **broadband** or **mobile broadband**.

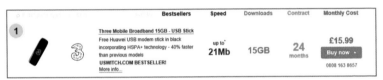

	Bestsellers	Speed	Downloads	Contract	Monthly Cost
1	**Three Mobile Broadband 15GB - USB Stick** Free Huawei USB modem stick in black incorporating HSPA+ technology - 40% faster than previous models USWITCH.COM BESTSELLER! More info...	up to* **21Mb**	15GB	24 months	£15.99 Buy now › 0808 163 8657

Once you've signed up for a contract, if using a telephone landline, within a few days the line will be activated for broadband. If you live in an area with the latest *fibre optic* cables you can receive extremely fast broadband such as *BT Infinity*. Your Internet Service Provider should provide a free router and all the necessary accessories, software and passwords to get the router up and running. If necessary the ISP may provide an engineer to set the router up for you. Finally the tablet, laptop or desktop computer(s) are connected wirelessly to the router using the wireless network adaptor built in or attached to each computer. This process is discussed shortly.

If you are connecting a computer to a mobile phone network you can either use pay-as-you go or take out a contract. It should just be a case of plugging in the dongle or SIM card and launching your Web browser such as Internet Explorer.

Setting up a router and mobile broadband are discussed in more detail in my book "Basic Computing for the Older Generation" ISBN 9780859347310 from Bernard Babani (publishing) Ltd.

The Web Browser

Windows 8 includes its own Web browser, Internet Explorer 10. The Web browser, together with a search program such as Bing or Google, allows you to find, display and navigate between Web pages. The browser also keeps a list of favourite Web sites. Internet Explorer appears as a tile on the Windows 8 Start Screen as shown on the right.

Tap or click the Internet Explorer tile to start surfing the Internet. Type *keywords* of interest such as **green woodpecker**, for example, into the **Bing** search bar, as shown below.

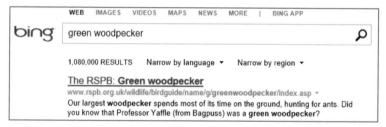

Or enter a Web address such as **www.babanibooks.com** into the black address bar at the bottom. These topics are discussed in detail in the next chapter.

Although Internet Explorer includes the Bing *search engine*, many people use the freely available Google program, as discussed in the next chapter.

Windows 8 includes the Internet Explorer Web browser by default. Some people believe this gives Microsoft and Internet Explorer an unfair advantage over other browsers. While the general user should find Internet Explorer meets their browsing needs, some advanced users prefer to use alternatives such as Google Chrome and Mozilla Firefox.

Making the Connection

This section describes the steps needed to connect a computer to a WiFi network. This might be a wireless router in your home or an access point in a public place such as a hotel or restaurant, etc. Each computer must have an Internet adaptor and Web browser software. If necessary the Internet connectivity in a tablet or laptop should be switched on. In the case of a home network, the router should be connected by a cable to a telephone line which has been activated for broadband by an Internet Service Provider such as BT. The router connects to the telephone socket through a *filter* which has two sockets, one for the router and one for the telephone handset. This allows the Internet and an ordinary telephone to be used at the same time.

Detecting the Router or Internet Access Point

Switch on the computer and enter your password to open the Windows 8 Start Screen. Swipe in from the right edge or click in the bottom right-hand corner of the screen to display the Charms Bar, as discussed in Chapter 2. Then tap or click the **Settings** charm shown on the right. You should see the following displayed at the bottom right of the screen.

The WiFi icon shown on the right and on the top left of the previous screenshot indicates that network connections are available. In the home situation this should include your router and possibly some of your neighbours' networks if they are within the WiFi range. Depending on  your equipment, this might be up to 150 feet indoors or 300 feet outdoors. An Internet access point in a public place would be detected in a similar way. Tap or click the icon shown above to list the available networks, as shown below.

In the example above, **BTHomeHub2-SW...** is our own BT router while **Livebox-E8A7** belongs to a neighbour. These routers must be up and running and within WiFi range. **Flight mode** above must be **Off** to connect to the Internet. It is switched on and off by tapping or clicking the small rectangle shown above next to **Off**. Flight mode **On** prevents the transmission of radio signals, which could interfere with an aircraft's systems. With Flight mode **On** you can still use the computer for non-Internet activities like music or word processing.

Connecting to the Router

Tap or click the name of your router in your list of routers, similar to the list on the previous page. You are then asked for a *security key*, often a string of numbers and letters stamped or printed on the back of the router. Without the protection of the security key anyone within WiFi range could detect and connect to your router and possibly access the information on any of the computers on your home network. For this reason you should always use a router which requires a security key.

After selecting your own router and entering the security key, tap or click **Connect** to complete the Internet connection. There is also a box to tick if you wish to connect to the Internet automatically at the start of every computing session. The word **Connected** now appears against your chosen router, as shown on the right.

Now, whenever you select the **Settings** charm, the name of your router, **BTHomeHub2-SW8N** in this example, should appear as shown on the right and below.

Troubleshooting

After using routers and network adaptors for a number of years, we have had very few problems in setting up the equipment or with the reliability of the connections to the Internet. However, you may suffer the odd glitch from time to time. This is indicated by the **Unavailable** note and white cross in a red circle on the WiFi icon as shown on the right.

Possible causes of this problem are:

- Some computers have an Internet switch and this may be turned off. This may be a physical switch. On my laptop the F2 function key is used as the Internet switch.

- The computer may use an Internet adaptor in the form of a USB dongle and there may be a bad connection or the adaptor is unplugged.

- **Flight mode**, as discussed earlier, is turned **On** in the **Settings** feature. Flight mode prevents Internet access.

- The cables between the router, the filter and the telephone socket are not properly connected.

- There may be a problem with the telephone line between your home and the telephone exchange. The further you are from the exchange, the weaker the broadband signal.

- Your Internet Service Provider may be carrying out maintenance work on their network.

- If you are upgrading to Windows 8 from an earlier version such as Windows XP, you might find some compatibility problems. If your computer has a network adaptor dongle you might find (as we did) that your Windows XP network adaptor is not compatible with Windows 8.

Overcoming Internet Connection Problems

Here are a few suggestions if you have trouble making the connection to the Internet:

- Make sure the Internet switch on your computer is in the **On** position (if applicable).

- Check that **Flight mode** is switched off.

- Check your router's handbook. The diagnostic lights should tell you if the broadband and WiFi are working.

- Router problems can often be solved by switching the router off for a few minutes and then switching it back on.

- Similarly, if you are using a network adaptor dongle, try removing the dongle for a short time before refitting it.

- Check that all cables are correctly connected.

- If you have a plug-in wireless network adaptor, make sure it is compatible with Windows 8. (Windows 7 adaptors should work with Windows 8). A new network adaptor dongle can be bought for a few pounds.

You can see what network adaptor is fitted to your computer (even if it is built-in during manufacture) by opening the Control Panel. This can be done quickly from the Windows 8 Start Screen by typing the first few letters such as **con** then tapping or clicking **Control Panel** in the rectangle, as shown on the right above.

Alternatively swipe in from the top or bottom edge (or right-click the mouse with the cursor over the Start Screen background). Then tap or click the **All apps** icon and select **Control Panel**.

Then select **Hardware and Sound**, **Device Manager** and **Network adaptors**. Our wireless network adaptor is listed below.

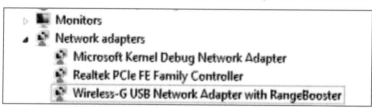

If you tap twice or double-click the name of your adaptor, you can find more information about the adaptor and its status — working or otherwise. If necessary download the latest software *drivers* to make it work with Windows 8.

Internet Speed

The various Internet Service Providers include broadband speed in their advertisements. The figures quoted are usually the *download* speeds for transmitting data from the Internet to your computer. This is particularly important if you want to download large files such as videos, photo collections and music and for streaming "catchup" television using BBC iPlayer, etc.

Broadband speed is usually quoted in *megabits per second* or *Mbps* or simply *Mb*. (Bits are binary digits, the 0s and 1s used to represent letters, etc., in the computer.) The minimum download speed for a service to be classed as broadband is 2Mb. Typical broadband speeds advertised at the time of writing range from 8 to 70Mb. In practice your actual speed may be considerably less.

The actual broadband speed achieved depends on a number of factors. Some remote areas of Britain can't receive broadband at all, while others have the very latest fibre optic cables. Distance from your telephone exchange is also a factor. In the future, fibre cables from the exchange to the cabinet (often green) in your road (FTTC) promise speeds of up to 40 Mb. In the longer term, fibre cables from the telephone exchange all the way to your home (FTTH) are forecast to give speeds of 100Mb or more.

Checking Your Broadband Speed

Type "**Broadband speed**" or similar into a search program such as Bing or Google. You'll find several links to speed test programs. These measure your download and upload speeds. The results of a test on our broadband service are shown below.

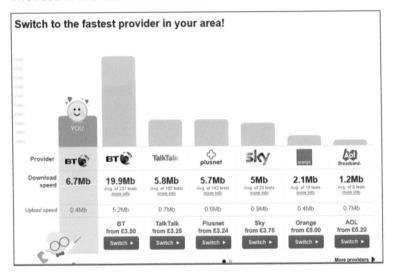

Switch to the fastest provider in your area!

Provider	BT	BT	TalkTalk	plusnet	sky	orange	AOL Broadband
Download speed	6.7Mb	19.9Mb Avg. of 237 tests more info	5.8Mb Avg. of 192 tests more info	5.7Mb Avg. of 143 tests more info	5Mb Avg. of 28 tests more info	2.1Mb Avg. of 19 tests more info	1.2Mb Avg. of 8 tests more info
Upload speed	0.4Mb	5.2Mb	0.7Mb	0.6Mb	0.9Mb	0.4Mb	0.7Mb
		BT from £3.50 Switch ►	TalkTalk from £3.25 Switch ►	Plusnet from £3.24 Switch ►	Sky from £3.75 Switch ►	Orange from £5.00 Switch ►	AOL from £5.20 Switch ►

More providers ►

As shown above in the **YOU** column on the extreme left, our download speed is 6.7Mb, in line with the British average of 7Mb. The uSwitch speed test above also gives details of alternative broadband services in our area. As shown above, it appears that a BT service of 20Mb is available in our road. This is the BT Infinity fibre optic service and although we live near to the telephone exchange our road doesn't have the necessary fibre cables. You can check the maximum BT broadband speed you can receive by opening the BT Web site **at www.bt.com** and entering your telephone number in the BT Infinity section.

Broadband option	Broadband speed range	Earliest you could get it
BT Total Broadband ⑦	Between 7.5Mb and 17.5Mb (Estimated speed: 13.0Mb)	Now

Connecting Printers

Previous pages have shown how a single wireless router can be used to connect one or more computers to the Internet using wireless technology. The computers can also be set up to "see" other computers on the home network and transfer files such as text documents and photographs. Once set up, this is quicker than alternative file transfer methods such as copying them to a removable flash drive or e-mailing the files to yourself.

Similarly the wireless home network can be used to allow several computers scattered around your home to send output to a single printer. Or you can have more than one printer on the home network and select whichever is best for the job in hand.

Detecting a Printer

If you are setting up a printer for the first time, it needs to be connected to a computer using a USB cable. If it is a wireless printer the cable may still be needed during the initial setup process. When connecting a computer to a printer on a wireless network, the printer needs to be online, up and running and not in *sleep mode*.

Open the **Control Panel** as discussed at the bottom of page 34. From the **Control Panel** select the green heading **Hardware and Sound**. On the next window select **Advanced printer setup** under **Devices and Printers**.

Windows then searches for available printers. If it finds more than one, select the printer you wish to connect to and then tap or click **Next**.

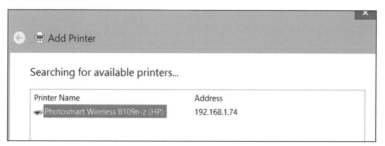

Windows will then search the Internet for the necessary *device* drivers, i.e. software to enable the printer to work with Windows 8. If necessary you may have to use the CD or DVD which came with the printer. Alternatively it may be necessary to log on to the printer manufacturer's Web site and download a suitable driver.

All being well you should see a note like the following, giving you the chance to print a test page.

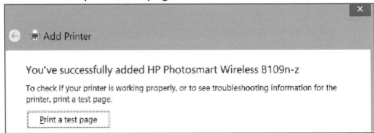

Select **Finish** and the printer should be ready to use.

To check on your printer at any time, select **Control Panel/ Hardware and Sound/View Devices and Printers**. The printer icon with a tick against it is the default printer. This will be used automatically whenever you print from within a program, such as Microsoft Word or Excel.

The **Devices and Printers** window can be used to check on the status of a printer and cancel any troublesome print jobs. Press and hold or right-click the printer icon to display a shortcut printer menu. This includes changing the default printer. Double tap or double click the printer icon to display printer status information.

Using the Internet

Introduction

Internet Explorer is a *Web browser*, a program or app used to navigate the enormous number of pages of information stored on millions of computers around the world. Internet Explorer has for many years been supplied with the Microsoft Windows operating system used in the majority of computers in the world. Manufacturers of rival Web browsers felt this gave Microsoft an unfair advantage. For this reason, Microsoft have been forced to offer a *Browser Choice Window* delivered through Windows Update and allowing you to install alternative Web browsers such as Google Chrome and Mozilla Firefox.

However, Internet Explorer has been used by many millions of people over the years and version 10 in Windows 8 and Windows RT has been well received, being very fast and with many innovative features. The majority of users should find that Internet Explorer 10 fulfils all of their requirements.

Some of the main functions of a Web browser are:

- To find and display Web pages containing specified information, after entering keywords into a *search engine* (program) such as Bing or Google.

- To open Web sites after their unique addresses are typed into the Address Bar in the browser.

- To navigate between different Web pages using *hyperlinks* built into the pages and also forward and back buttons and *tabs*.

- To save links or bookmarks allowing you to return to *favourite* or recently visited Web sites.

The Keyword Search
Using the Bing Search Engine

The range of subjects and depth of information available on the Internet is amazing. In my experience you can find up-to-date information on any subject under the sun. For example, suppose you want to find out about the red squirrel. From the Start Screen tap or click the **Internet Explorer** tile, shown on the right.

Then enter **red squirrel** in the Bing search bar, as shown below.

When you tap or click the **Web Search** button shown above you will see a list of search results almost instantly, as shown below.

In this example there are millions of results, but the most relevant ones are usually near the top of the list. The list of results can be reduced considerably, e.g. by selecting **Narrow by region** as shown on the previous page and then choosing **UK** for example. Also many of the results will contain the words **red** and **squirrel** on the page but not together, as in "a grey **squirrel** was chasing a **red** admiral". These unwanted results can be eliminated by entering the keywords in quotation marks, i.e. **"red squirrel"**.

To look at a Web page that interests you, tap or click its link in the list of search results, such as:

BBC Nature - **Red squirrel** videos, news and facts
www.bbc.co.uk › ... › Rodents › Squirrels › Bushy-tailed squirrels
Instantly recognisable by their red fur, ear tufts and long, fluffy tails, red squirrels were once the only squirrel species in Europe.

The underlined text above is a link to the BBC Nature Web site. Tap or click the link to open the Web page, as shown below.

Upper and Lower Case Letters in Keywords

It doesn't usually matter whether you enter keywords in upper or lower case letters — **samuel johnson** yields the same results as **Samuel Johnson** or even **SAMUEL JOHNSON**.

The Google Search Engine

Bing, discussed on the previous two pages, is the search engine included with the Windows 8 and Windows RT operating systems. However, the Google search engine has for many years been an extremely popular program for carrying out keyword searches. Google is free and can be opened by entering **www.google.co.uk** into the Address Bar at the bottom of the Internet Explorer 10 screen, as discussed in more detail shortly.

The Google Search Bar is shown on the right in the centre. Keywords are entered here in a similar way to that described on the previous pages for Bing. Searches can be narrowed down by  selecting a category such as **Images**, **Maps** or **News**, etc.

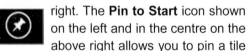

Pinning a Tile for a Web Site to the Start Screen

To the right of the Address Bar at the bottom of the Internet Explorer 10 screen there are several tools, as shown on the  right. The **Pin to Start** icon shown 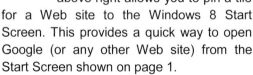 on the left and in the centre on the above right allows you to pin a tile  for a Web site to the Windows 8 Start Screen. This provides a quick way to open Google (or any other Web site) from the Start Screen shown on page 1.

Using a Web Address

Most companies, organisations and many individuals now have their own Web site, to publish news and information. Each Web site is identified on the Internet by a unique address or *URL* (*Uniform Resource Locator*). Many organisations include their address on their correspondence or on their vehicles, for example:

www.babanibooks.com

The Web address gives a very quick way to move directly to a particular Web site, without having to peruse a list of search results, as with the keyword search.

From the Start Screen shown on page 1, tap or click the Internet tile, as shown on the right. The Internet Explorer 10 page opens, as shown below. For normal browsing the Web page occupies the whole of the screen. However, if you swipe up from the bottom or down from the top, or right click a mouse, the black toolbars appear across the top and bottom, as shown below.

Tap or click the Address Bar at the bottom of the screen and enter the new Web address to replace the previous address, as shown below.

When you tap or press **Enter**, the required Web site is quickly displayed.

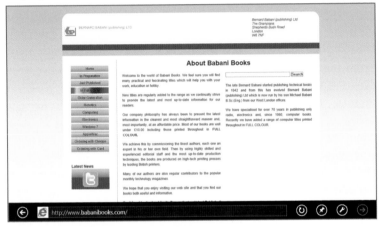

Navigating Around a Web Site

Within most Web pages there are a number of *links* or *hyperlinks*, usually in the form of text or images. If you pass a cursor over a link, the cursor changes to a hand. Tapping or clicking the link opens another page on the Web site or opens another Web site. Circled arrows at the extreme left and right of the taskbar at the bottom of the Web page as shown below allow you to move forward and back through previously visited pages.

The functions of the other three icons above on the right are described at the top of the next page.

This icon refreshes the Web page with the latest up-to-date information.

 Tapping or clicking this icon displays options to create or pin a tile for the current Web page on the Start Screen or on Favorites as discussed shortly.

 This icon has options to search for and highlight certain words in a long document. You can also view a Web page in the traditional Windows Desktop

Returning to Web Pages

To return to Web sites at a later time, tap or click anywhere in the Internet Explorer 10 Address Bar. Tiles for previously visited sites appear as shown below. On the left below are the Web sites you have **Pinned** to the Start Screen. In the middle there are tiles which Windows has classified as **Frequent**. On the right below are any Web pages you have designated as **Favourites**.

The three **Pinned** Web pages on the left of Internet Explorer 10 above appear on the right of the Start Screen, as shown on the right below.

Tap or click a tile to quickly open a previously visited Web site.

Tabbed Browsing

Tabs allow you to have several Web sites open at a time and move easily between them.

With a Web site open in Internet Explorer 10, swipe in from the top or bottom or right-click a mouse. Tap or click the **New Tab** icon shown on the right and on the top right on the main screenshot below.

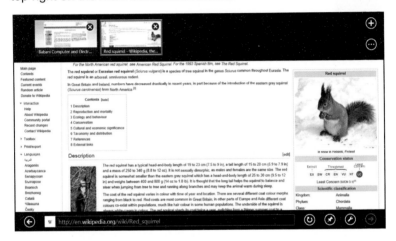

Now open another Web site either by a keyword search or by entering its address in the Address Bar of Internet Explorer 10, as discussed earlier in this chapter. The new Web site opens with its own tab, as shown below.

To switch between Web sites simply tap or click the tab or thumbnail image of the page. To close a Web site tap or click the cross on the tab.

The Windows Store

When you first begin using Windows 8 and RT, the Start Screen already displays a lot of tiles, representing apps or programs. These are included by default in a new installation of Windows. As discussed earlier, you may also have tiles for apps and Web sites which you have pinned to the Start Screen yourself.

The default tiles include popular apps such as News, Weather, the Internet, People, SkyDrive, Camera, Mail, Maps, Photos, the Desktop, Music and Video. In addition the Store tile allows you to browse thousands of apps which have been specially designed to work with the Modern UI (user interface) or Start Screen in Windows 8 and Windows RT, as shown above. Apps are available in a wide variety of categories such as health, music, entertainment, education, business, sport, books, food and lifestyle. New apps are continually being designed and added to the Store. Many apps are free to download to your computer while others may cost a few pounds.

When you download an app, you become the owner of that app. It appears as a tile on your Start Screen and initially is only installed on the computer used to download it. However, you are allowed to install an app on up to 5 different computers.

The Windows Store is opened by tapping or clicking its tile on the Start Screen as shown on the right.

The Windows Store opens and you can scroll through thousands of apps, some arranged under tiles representing broad category headings such as **News & Weather** or **Sport**.

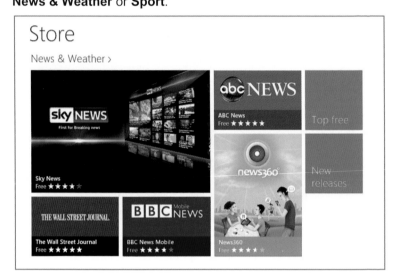

Other tiles in the Windows Store represent a single app, such as the well-known search engine Google and the online auction house eBay. There is also an app for the free Skype Internet telephone service, discussed later in this book. These new apps make it easier to use the services from within the Modern UI. Sample tiles for some well-known apps in the Windows Store are shown below.

The range of apps covers most aspects of life, such as help with medical matters in the **Health Choices** app, which gives information about NHS services.

Downloading and Installing an App

Although the Amazon Kindle is well-known as a stand-alone device for reading books electronically, you can download a Kindle app. This turns your Windows 8 or Windows RT tablet, laptop or desktop computer into an e-book reader. Scroll through the Windows Store to find the **Books & Reference** section. Tap or click the **Books & Reference** heading and then select **Kindle**, as shown on the right and on the lower right below.

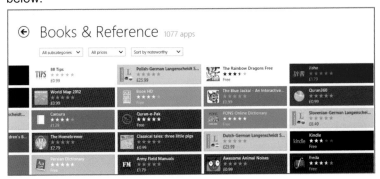

You are then presented with a description of the app, as follows.

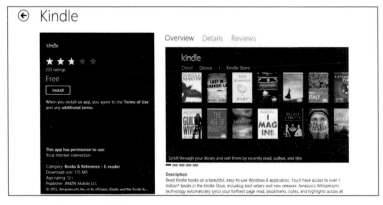

Now tap or click **Install**, shown above. If there is a charge for the app you will have to supply your name and address and credit card details. etc. The app is downloaded to your computer in a few seconds and a tile appears on your Start Screen. In this example, the tile for the new Kindle app is shown on the right, together with three other newly-installed apps from the Windows Store. Tap or click the tile on the Start Screen to launch the Kindle app, as shown below.

Internet Security

By enabling millions of computers to communicate with each other around the world, the Internet has created opportunities in work, education, communication and entertainment, etc., that previous generations could never have imagined. Unfortunately, in addition to these legitimate activities, the Internet provides skilful *hackers* with opportunities for a range of criminal acts. Unlike conventional crime, there is no burglary or violence and the criminal may be thousands of miles from the crime scene — which might be the computer in your home.

A major type of Internet crime is *malware*, i.e. malicious software. This is the use of specially written programs designed to damage or invade your computer and its files. These include *viruses*, *worms* and *Trojan horses*. Viruses may be attached to e-mails or software and are designed to spread, cause damage to files and slow down computer systems and networks. Worms can spread without being attached to a program. The Trojan Horse poses as a legitimate piece of software but has an illegal purpose such as to give a hacker access to your computer. *Spyware* uses *phishing* to try to find out personal and financial information, such as your bank account details.

Windows 8 and Windows RT provide a wide range of security software to combat these threats. These are turned on by default but it's worth checking they are up and running and up-to-date.

Open the Control Panel, as discussed on page 45, and under **System and Security**, select **Review your computer's status**. In the **Action Center** shown below, tap or click the arrow to the right of the word **Security**.

This displays a drop-down list of the main security tools and their status, **On** or **Off**, as shown below.

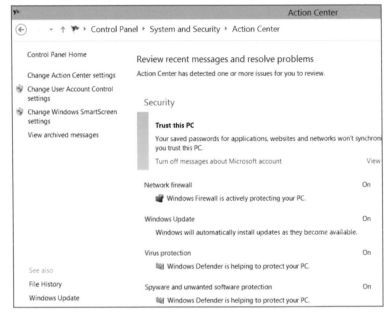

To change the **On** or **Off** status of any of the security messages, tap or click **Change Action Center settings** shown at the top left of the **Action Center** shown above. Then tap or click the check box to add or remove a tick from a security tool.

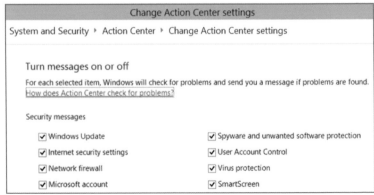

Windows Firewall

The **Windows Firewall** shown on the previous page is a barrier designed to stop hackers and malicious software such as worms from entering your computer. The firewall can also prevent malware being sent out from a computer to the Internet.

Windows Update

Windows Update downloads and installs the latest software upgrades from Microsoft, frequently intended to fix security problems. This is usually done automatically or you may be asked to choose whether or not to install a particular update. The Browser Choice window (discussed earlier) may be downloaded as a Windows Update. A log of all your recent updates is kept in the **update history** shown below. This is displayed after selecting **Windows Update** at the bottom left of the **Action Center** shown at the top of the previous page. Then tap or click **View update history** at the top left of the **Windows Update** window.

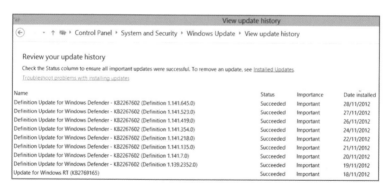

Many of the updates downloaded by Windows Update are *virus definitions*. These allow anti-virus software such as Windows Defender to detect and eradicate the latest viruses. Windows Defender is listed in the Action Center at the top of the previous page and discussed on the next page.

Windows Defender

This software is included in Windows 8 and RT and should always be **On**, as previously discussed. The window shown below can be quickly launched by swiping up from the bottom of the Start Screen or right

clicking to display the **All apps** icon shown on the above right. Then scroll across the All apps screen and tap or click **Windows Defender** or its icon.

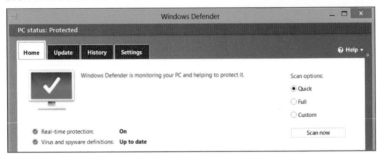

Windows Defender continually monitors your computer for viruses, spyware and malware. You can also launch a manual scan whenever you wish, using **Scan now** shown in the bottom right-hand corner above. Viruses are continually being developed, so the latest virus and spyware definitions are regularly updated automatically to Defender.

SmartScreen

The SmartScreen feature detects suspicious e-mails, etc., from unknown sources which can't be detected by normal antimalware software. SmartScreen Filter issues alerts about unsafe Web sites which may be "phishing" for your bank details, etc.

Electronic Mail

This was one of the first popular applications of the Internet and remains extremely important in both social and business situations. Although *social networking* Web sites like Facebook and Twitter (discussed in the next chapter) provide exciting new methods of communication, *e-mail* has some advantages.

E-mail replaces the letter sent in the post between friends, family and business contacts. Some advantages of e-mail are:

- The message is delivered to its destination almost instantly. It is then immediately available to be read.

- The same message can be sent to many recipients, easily selected from an electronic address book.

- It is very simple for recipients to *reply* or *forward* the message to someone else.

- An e-mail can have large files attached, such as text documents, spreadsheets, video clips or photographs.

- Messages can easily be deleted or saved in an organised structure of folders, for future reference.

- E-mail can be used for long messages. Social networks like Twitter are limited to very short messages.

Electronic mail might be used to communicate with long-lost relatives around the world, including the exchange of photographs. Documents, photographs and other files are "clipped" (metaphorically speaking) to the message and are known as *attachments*. The text in the main body of the e-mail can be quite lengthy or it may simply be a covering note for any attachments. If you want a friend to see a particular Web site, you can embed a *link* to the Web site in the e-mail. Your friend simply taps or clicks the link to launch the Web site.

The Windows Mail App

Windows 8 and Windows RT have their own e-mail app, known as *Windows Mail* or simply *Mail*. This is launched by tapping or clicking its tile on the Start Screen, shown in the extract below.

In the example below, I have sent a test e-mail to myself. The **1** at the bottom right of the tile is a *notification* of a new message.

Tap or click the tile to open the **Mail** window. The main body of the e-mail is shown below.

Jim Gatenby 06 December 2012 11:51
Just a test
To: Jim Gatenby

You can send a copy of an e-mail to yourself to check what your contact will receive.

Sent from my Windows 8 PC

The E-mail Address

In order to send and receive e-mails you need a unique e-mail address such as:

stellajohnson@hotmail.com

Windows 8 and Windows RT use your Microsoft e-mail address to sign in to the Lock Screen, to access the Windows Store and to share information with sites such as Facebook and Twitter.

Creating a New Microsoft Account

From the **Settings** charm discussed in Chapter 2, select **Change PC settings** and **Users** then **Add a user**. You can use an existing address or click **Sign up for a new e-mail address** to create a new Microsoft account, as shown below.

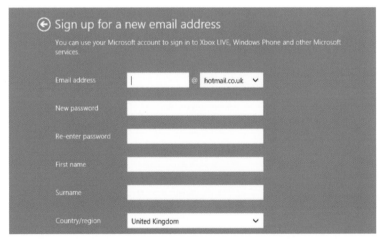

Enter your chosen name in front of **@hotmail.com** shown above. Once you've signed up for a new e-mail address you can start using it to send and receive messages in **Mail**. If you've had a Microsoft account before (with Windows 7, say), this address can be used with Mail and other apps in Windows 8 and RT.

After you've signed in to the Lock Screen discussed in Chapter 1, tap or click the **Mail** tile on the Start Screen, shown on the right. The **Mail** window opens displaying the **Inbox**, as shown below.

Down the left-hand side are various folders, such as the **Inbox**, **Drafts**, **Sent Items**, **Outbox**, **Junk** and **Deleted items**. Tap or click to open a folder.

Receiving an E-Mail

The messages you receive are listed in the centre panel of the Inbox with the sender's name, subject and time, as shown below.

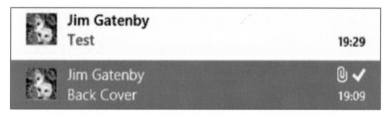

The tick on the lower message above shows that the message has been read. The paperclip icon denotes that this message includes an attachment such as a document or photograph.

Tap or click the listing of the message to open it for reading in the right-hand panel, as shown on the next page.

Jim Gatenby 06 December 2012 19:09
Back Cover
To: Jim Gatenby

 Back cover Facebook
doc 57.0 KB

Mike

Please find attached the text for the back cover of our latest book.

At the top left are the sender's name and the date and time of sending. The name next to **To:** above should be the real recipient's name rather than mine used in this dummy test. The two owl chicks are my account picture, as discussed in Chapter 3, but you may prefer to leave your account picture blank or include an actual picture of yourself with the e-mails you send.

The three icons on the right and also shown above are (reading from left to right) for starting a *new* message, *replying* to a message and *deleting* a message.

The Attachment

The icon shown on the right and above is an attachment, in this case a document produced in the Word program. Tap or click the icon to produce a menu to open or

 Back cover Facebook
.doc 57.0 KB

save the file. If you select **Open**, the document will open in its associated program such as Microsoft Word. Similarly a spreadsheet file might open in Microsoft Excel and a drawing or photo might open in Windows Paint. **Open with** lets you choose the program to use. **Save** lets you select a folder on your computer in which to save the attachment file.

Creating an E-mail

To create a new message, tap or click the **Mail** tile on the Start Screen shown earlier. Then tap or click the **New** icon shown on the right and on the previous page.

A new blank e-mail window opens ready for you to enter the text of the message. First enter the e-mail addresses of the main recipients in the **To:** slot, pressing **Enter** after each one.

The **Cc:** slot above is used to send a (carbon) copy to other people who may be interested. The small icons as shown on the right and on the right of the **To:** slot above are used to add people from your contacts list to the recipients of the new message. People are added to your contacts list automatically when you receive mail from them.

Next give a title to the message, replacing the words **Add a subject** shown above. It's now time to start entering the main body text under the horizontal line on the right-hand side shown above. Swipe in from the top or bottom or right click a mouse to display the formatting toolbar along the bottom of the screen, as shown below. The formatting features include different font styles, sizes and colour of letters and bold and italics, etc.

The above toolbar also appears when you highlight a piece of text.

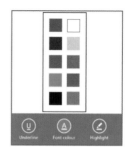

In the example below, the font style, size and colour have been set using the toolbar icons shown above.

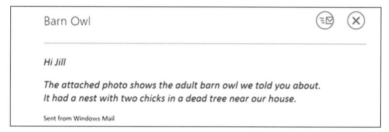

Barn Owl

Hi Jill

The attached photo shows the adult barn owl we told you about.
It had a nest with two chicks in a dead tree near our house.

Sent from Windows Mail

Emoticons are small images, often facial expressions, added to a message to show your feelings or perhaps add some humour.

If you tap or click the **Emoticons** icon shown on the right and at the bottom of the previous page, you are presented with a huge choice of images on different subjects to add to the main body of text in your e-mail.

Activities

Inserting an Attachment

If you wish to include a file such as a photo or text document, .
you need to know where the file has been saved, such as a folder
on your hard disc drive or on a removable flash drive. Open the
Mail toolbar on the screen by swiping in from the top or bottom or
right clicking with a mouse. Then tap
or click **Attachments** as shown on
the right. The **Files** window opens
allowing   you   to   browse   your
computer and its discs, flash drives, etc., for the required file.

When you tap or click to select a file to send with your e-mail, the
file is ticked, as shown above and the
Attach button at the bottom of the **Files**
window is highlighted, as shown on the
right.

Tap or click the **Attach** button and an icon or thumbnail image of
the document or photo appears on the left of the e-mail message,
as shown on the next page.

In the above screenshot the note **1 file attached** appears under the image. By default files are sent as e-mail attachments. In addition there is a note under the image saying **Send using SkyDrive instead**. This SkyDrive option is discussed shortly.

Sending an E-mail

The finished e-mail, complete with recipients' e-mail addresses, subject, body text and any attachments can now be sent by tapping or clicking the envelope icon shown on the right and near top right of the message window above. A copy of the message is temporarily placed in your **Outbox** until it has been actually sent. Then it will appear in your **Sent items** folder as shown below.

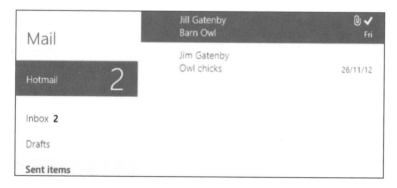

Responding to an E-mail

New messages are listed in the centre panel of your Inbox, with the sender's name, day or time and a paperclip icon if there are any attachments, as shown below.

Tap or click the e-mail header shown above to open the message and then tap or click the attachment thumbnail or icon.

Then select **Open**, **Open with** or **Save** from the menu shown above. In this example, **Open with** was selected to open a photo in the Windows Paint program, shown on the right. **Save** allows you to store a copy of the document or photo on your computer's hard disc, etc.

Having read the e-mail and looked at any attachments, you may wish to send a reply. Tap or click the **Respond** icon in the centre of the three icons shown on the right and on the previous page. **Reply** sends your reply to the original sender. **Reply all** sends your reply to the original sender and to everyone who

received the original message. Their e-mail addresses are entered automatically — you only need to enter the text of your reply. **Forward** is used to send on a copy of the original message to someone you think might be interested.

SkyDrive

Underneath the icon or thumbnail for an attachment in the New Message window is the note "**1 file attached Send using SkyDrive instead**". If you tap or click this note, a copy of the document or photo is sent to your SkyDrive "cloud" storage location on the Internet. As a user of Windows 8 or Windows RT you have your own SkyDrive storage space

of 7GB where you can send files. Bigger files can be sent to SkyDrive than can be sent as e-mail attachments.

You can access the files on SkyDrive from virtually any computer with an Internet connection, anywhere in the world. You can share SkyDrive files such as documents and photographs with other people by using the SkyDrive e-mail option above or by sending them a link to your SkyDrive folder.

There is a SkyDrive app with a tile on the Start Screen, as shown on the right. SkyDrive can also be accessed from the Web site at:

https://skydrive.live.com

Giving Someone Access to a File on SkyDrive

There are two ways to allow someone else to access photographs and documents on your SkyDrive.

Sending an E-mail Attachment Using the SkyDrive Option

Add the file as an attachment when creating a new e-mail. Then select **Send using SkyDrive instead** as discussed previously. When the recipient opens the message, an icon or thumbnail is displayed on the message. A link to SkyDrive appears underneath the thumbnail or photo as shown below, allowing the recipient to view the full document or photograph on SkyDrive.

Sending Someone a Link to Your SkyDrive

Open SkyDrive as shown below and browse to find the document or photograph you wish to send.

https://skydrive.live.com/   ✕

Tap or click the icon or thumbnail for the file and then select **Sharing** and **Share** in the right-hand panel. Enter the e-mail address of the recipient in the **To:** slot. Add a personal message if you wish. You can give the recipient permission to edit the document or photo on SkyDrive, if necessary for joint projects.

Finally tap or click the **Share** button to send the link on its way. The recipient only has to tap or click the **View Photo** link shown below to open the document or photograph, etc.

You are invited to view Jim's photo.

View photo

OLYMPUS DIGITAL CAMERA

Social Networking

Introduction

As discussed in the previous chapter, electronic mail was for many years the main method of communication between people across the Internet. However, recent years have seen the arrival of *social networking* Web sites designed to provide new ways for people to interact and exchange information. Some of the most popular (free) Web sites used for social networking, which have millions of users worldwide, are as follows:

Facebook

Users enter biographical information, including a Timeline of major life events. They may then become friends with like-minded people to exchange news and photographs, etc.

Twitter

This Web site allows you to post short text messages on the Internet. Users can choose to follow the messages of other people such as friends, family and celebrities. Twitter can also be used for online debates on popular subjects and causes.

LinkedIn

Professional people use this Web site to build up their contacts lists, to find out about employment opportunities and to provide prospective employers with their CVs, etc.

Skype

Although not a social networking Web site like Facebook and Twitter, Skype allows people to communicate using free voice and video calls between computers anywhere on the Internet.

The People App

At the time of writing the popular social networking sites Facebook and Twitter do not have specially designed apps with tiles on the Windows 8 Start Screen. However, as discussed shortly, Facebook and Twitter can be opened by typing their Web addresses into the address bar in Internet Explorer. You can also create tiles for Facebook and Twitter on the Start Screen so that you can open them with a single tap or click, as discussed shortly.

The People app is designed to integrate all your social networking contacts and has a tile on the Start Screen. The tile is a constantly changing display of images from your Facebook, Twitter and e-mail contacts, as shown on the right. The People app collects together all of the  people you interact with on the Internet on Facebook, Twitter, Email, Skype, etc. and sorts them into an alphabetical list. Tap or click the People tile to display the list, as shown below.

Tap or click **What's new** shown above to see a list of your friends' latest updates on Facebook or Twitter.

The Facebook Social Network

This is probably the most popular social networking site, with over a billion users. Although originally started by college students in America, it is now used by people of all ages. Facebook is becoming increasingly popular with older people especially if they have children and grandchildren on the other side of the world. Businesses and celebrities also use Facebook for promotional purposes, enabling them to reach a very large audience with their latest news and information.

Facebook Friends

Facebook is based around the concept of having lots of *friends*. These may include close personal friends and family but may also include people you have never met in the real world. Some people have thousands of "friends" on Facebook.

These virtual friends on Facebook are people with whom you have agreed to share news and information across the Internet. Facebook identifies people who you might want to invite to be your friends, perhaps because they are in the list of contacts in your e-mail address book and are already members of Facebook. When you join Facebook you can enter a personal profile giving details of your education, employment and interests, etc. This information allows Facebook to suggest people who you might want to invite to be a friend. They can either accept or decline this invitation.

Confidentiality and Security

Facebook provides a platform for you to post on the Internet a great deal of personal and biographical information. The Internet enables this information to be viewed by a potential audience of millions of people. Facebook has *privacy settings* to allow you to restrict the viewing of certain types of information to specific groups of people. It's advisable not to put confidential information on Facebook unless you are thoroughly conversant with the privacy settings. You are also advised not to accept complete strangers as Facebook friends or arrange to meet up with them.

Joining Facebook

Signing up to Facebook requires you to be at least 13 years of age, with a computer online to the Internet and a valid e-mail address. Enter **www.facebook.com** into the address bar of Internet Explorer, as shown below and discussed in Chapter 6.

The Facebook **Sign Up** screen appears as shown below.

From your e-mail address, Facebook checks your e-mail contacts for people who are already on Facebook. You can then invite them to be Facebook friends. Any e-mail contacts who are not members of Facebook may be sent an invitation to join.

Your Facebook Profile or Timeline

You are then asked to start entering your *Profile* information, also called your *Timeline*. The profile or timeline contains details such as your education, employment history, hobbies and interests and your address and contact details

You can also add a profile picture, allowing friends to identify you after a search on Facebook, which may have produced a lot of people with the same name as you. If you have a suitable profile picture stored on your computer, it can be uploaded to Facebook, after clicking **Upload a photo**, shown below. Otherwise, if you have a *webcam* on your computer, you can take a picture and upload it directly to Facebook using **Take a photo** shown below.

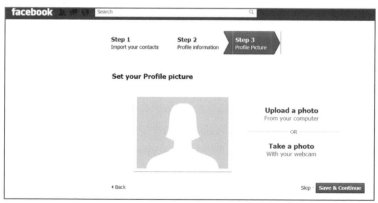

You don't have to fill in every part of your profile or timeline during the sign-up process — you can return to edit it later.

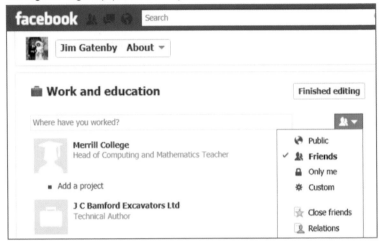

At the right of some of the personal information you enter is the *inline audience selector* icon shown on the right. Click this icon to open the menu shown above. This allows you to select the audience for the item of information, e.g. **Public**, **Friends** and **Only me**, etc.

Communicating With Others Via Your Wall

You can type text and add photos in the **Status** box shown below and **Post** updates to a "noticeboard" known as your **Wall**. Others can view your **Wall** according to the privacy settings such as **Friends** or **Close friends** on the menu shown below.

Tweeting with Twitter

Twitter is another very popular social network with over 200 million users worldwide. Although there are some similarities with Facebook, Twitter is also different in many ways.

What is a Tweet?

One of the main features of Twitter is that messages or *tweets* can be no more than 140 characters long. This makes Twitter suitable for brief text messages like SMS phone texts. As well as PC and Apple computers, Twitter can also be used on the latest smartphones such as the iPhone and the Blackberry.

Whereas e-mail messages are sent to the unique e-mail addresses of known contacts, tweets can be read by very large numbers of people who may be complete strangers to the tweeter. Twitter is based on the idea that users will want to follow the regular pronouncements of other people such as friends, family, celebrities, politicians, reporters or companies and other organisations.

Followers on Twitter

Regular tweeters may post messages several times a day, such as the actor and writer Stephen Fry, who has millions of *followers*. Some users of Twitter will be followers who only read other people's tweets, rather than posting their own. You need to be sufficiently well-known for lots of other people to want to read what you have to say in your tweets, or find ways of encouraging people to become your followers.

You can choose to follow anyone you like on Twitter, but you can't choose who follows you. You can read all the tweets of the people you follow and send a reply if you wish.

You may also be interested in our book Social Networking for the Older Generation (ISBN 9780859347341) from Bernard Babani (publishing) Ltd.

Signing up for Twitter

Log on to the Twitter Web site by entering the following in the address bar of your Web browser, such as Internet Explorer 10.

www.twitter.com

Fill in the box, shown on the right, including a valid e-mail address and a password. Then click **Sign up for Twitter**, as shown on the right. Your username, **@samueljohnson** for example, and Twitter account are then created. Then the Twitter Teacher gets you

started by providing a list of people for you to follow. When you click the **Follow** button against a person's name and picture, as shown below, their messages appear on your tweet page.

You can also search your e-mail address list for people to follow on Twitter. An image of yourself can be added with a short text profile. An e-mail is sent to you by Twitter and you click on a link for confirmation. You can now begin tweeting.

Hashtags

A hashtag is a word or phrase, etc., preceded by the hash sign (**#**) and placed in a tweet, e.g. **#BBCQT**. (BBC Question Time in this case). Clicking on a hashtag which appears in a tweet allows you to read all the tweets on that particular topic. You can also find all the relevant tweets by entering the hashtag in the search bar at the top of the Twitter screen as shown below.

Hashtags allow anyone on Twitter to participate in online forums on current news issues or television programs, for example.

Twitter in Use

Whereas Facebook relies heavily on detailed personal profiles to bring together people sharing similar backgrounds and interests, Twitter only accepts about a paragraph of biographical information, as shown below under **findmypast.co.uk**.

Many companies, such as the family history Web site, **findmypast.co.uk**, include a link to Twitter on their main Web site. Clicking this link opens the Twitter Home page of **findmypast.co.uk** as shown below.

Posting a Tweet

Start Twitter by entering **www.twitter.com** in the address bar of your Web browser such as Internet Explorer 10. Sign on to Twitter with your username and password then type your message in the box under **What's happening**. The number **99** shown on the lower right below is the number of characters still available to be used out of the maximum of 140. (You don't have to use all 140 characters).

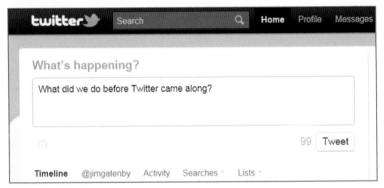

Click the Tweet button shown above to post the tweet.

Reading Tweets

The message is posted and is immediately available on the *timeline* or list of tweets of anyone following you, as shown below. This shows a tweet posted one minute previously by me to anyone following me. My username **@jimgatenby** is shown below. In this case the follower is Christopher Walls, username **@christowalls** — the change in spelling needed because the full name was already taken by another Twitter user.

Creating Tiles for Facebook and Twitter

Open Internet Explore 10 from its tile on the Start Screen. Launch **Facebook** or **Twitter** by typing their Web address such as **www.facebook.com** or **www.twitter.com** into the address bar as previously described. Then swipe in from the top or bottom or right click with the mouse to display the toolbar shown below and at the bottom of the Facebook Sign Up screen in Internet Explorer shown on page 94.

Tap or click the pin icon shown on the right and above to open the small window containing the **Pin to Start** button shown below.

After you tap or click **Pin to Start** shown below on the right a tile for Twitter or Facebook is placed on the Start Screen.

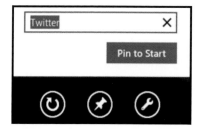

Facebook and Twitter can now be launched by tapping or clicking their respective tiles on the Start Screen, as shown below.

Skype

This is an Internet service which allows you to make free voice and video calls between computers. For example, you could see and speak to friends or relatives In New Zealand in real time without running up a phone bill. All you (both) need is a computer connected to the Internet, equipped with a microphone and speakers. For a video call you also need a webcam on each machine. The latest tablet and laptop computers have all these accessories built-in from new. If necessary, especially on desktop machines, these devices can be bought separately for a few pounds and simply plugged in, ready to use straightaway.

There is a Skype app for Windows 8 and RT, available from the Windows Store. This is free and can be downloaded after tapping or clicking the Store tile on the Start Screen shown on the right. Then scroll across the Store and tap or click the **Skype** tile shown on the right. This opens the description window shown below including an **Install** button. When you select the **Install** button a tile for launching Skype is placed on the Start Screen of the Modern UI.

Creating a New Skype Name and Password

The e-mail names and addresses in your People feature as discussed earlier are used as your Skype contacts list. You are signed in to Skype automatically using the e-mail address and password for your Microsoft account. To create a new Skype account you need to create a new Microsoft User account in **Change PC settings**, on the **Settings** charm, as discussed on page 81. When Skype opens, your People contacts are listed in the right-hand panel as shown at the bottom of the previous page. Tap or click the required contact to see if they're **available**, as shown on the right in the blue area. Tap or click the left-hand icon to make a video call using a webcam or select the middle icon

to make a voice only call. Tap or click the right-hand plus icon above to allow others to join the conversation. After you tap or click to make a call, your contact (if online), will hear the dial tone and can tap or click their green phone icon to accept the call.

If your contact is not online when you call, you can use Skype on your computer to call a mobile phone or landline. Unlike calls between two computers on the Internet, there is a charge for these calls, for which you need credit in your Skype account.

During a video call, the participants should be visible to each other and the following icons are displayed:

These icons represent a webcam (video call), microphone (mute/unmute), instant messaging and the red icon used to end a call.

Tidying Up The Start Screen

When you install apps from the Windows Store, tiles are pinned to the Start Screen. You may also pin some of your favourite Web sites to the Start Screen as tiles. Eventually you may have some old tiles you wish to get rid of, as described below.

Touchscreen Operation

Drag the tile slightly downwards until a small tick appears at the top right of the tile. A toolbar appears, as shown lower down this page.

Mouse

Right-click the tile and the tick appears in the top right corner as shown above, with the toolbar displayed as shown below.

Keyboard

Use the cursor (arrow) keys to move over and highlight the required tile and then press the space bar. The tick should appear in the top right-hand corner of the tile as shown above.

The number of icons on the toolbar varies according to the type of tile. A tile which is a link to a Web site just has an **Unpin from Start** icon. A tile for an app also has an **Uninstall** icon on the toolbar. A large size tile has a **Smaller** icon to halve its size. A small tile for an app has a **Larger** icon. A live tile which changes regularly has a **Turn live tile off** icon, as shown below.

Rearranging Tiles

You can move tiles to new positions by dragging with your finger or by holding down the left mouse button. Dragging tiles to the right enables you to create a separate block of your own tiles.

Essential Differences: Windows 8 & RT

Previous chapters of this book have shown that Windows 8 and RT are superficially almost identical. The only real differences are in the ways you obtain or install each operating system and the applications or programs which are compatible and can be run on each system. The important differences are as follows:

- You cannot upgrade a computer to run Windows RT – Windows RT is only supplied on new computers with ARM processors, such as the Microsoft Surface tablet.

- Windows 8 (basic) is known as an OEM version (Original Equipment Manufacturer), intended only for builders of new computers. OEM versions are not intended to be installed by ordinary consumers.

- Windows 8 Pro is intended for consumers wishing to upgrade computers running earlier versions of Windows such as Windows XP, Vista and Windows 7. Windows 8 Pro can be installed on PC tablet, laptop and desktop computers using x86 Intel or AMD processors.

- Windows 8 Pro is available as a download from the Microsoft Web site. A more expensive version on DVD is also available from Microsoft and other retailers.

If you don't relish the task of upgrading your old computer you might get a local computer shop or someone else to do it. Alternatively, if funds allow, buy a new computer with Windows 8, Windows 8 Pro or Windows RT already installed.

Upgrading to Windows 8 Pro

In order to upgrade to Windows 8 Pro your computer must be running Windows XP (with Service Pack 3), Windows Vista, Windows 7, Windows 8 Consumer Preview or Windows 8 Release Preview. On computers running Windows 7 or the Preview editions your files and apps (programs) remain in place after the installation of Windows 8 Pro. If your PC is running Windows XP or Vista your apps will need to be reinstalled from the original media on which they were supplied, such as DVDs.

System Requirements

Computers made in recent years should be capable of running Windows 8 Pro. Microsoft recommend the following specification:

I GHz processor or faster

2GB RAM (main memory)

20GB hard disc space

1366x768 screen resolution

DirectX 9 graphics

To use touch operation you need a tablet computer or a laptop, desktop or hybrid computer with a touch-sensitive screen.

32-bit or 64-bit

The Windows 8 Pro boxed package includes a 32-bit DVD and a 64-bit DVD. The 64-bit version works faster but not all computers can run it. To find out if your computer can run the 64-bit version, select **Control Panel**, **System and Security**, **System**, **Performance Information and Tools** and **View and print detailed performance system and information**. It should say "**64-bit capable Yes**" if your computer can run the 64-bit version of Windows 8. If in doubt the software documentation advises users to install the 32-bit version initially.

Downloading the Windows 8 Pro Upgrade

This method installs Windows 8 Pro on a computer currently running Windows XP, Vista or Windows 7. If your machine is running Windows XP or Vista you will need the original media for your apps so that you can reinstall them on Windows 8.

Clear instructions appear on the screen at every stage, so you should be able to accomplish this task even if you are new to computing. Log on to the Windows 8 Download page after entering the address **http://windows.microsoft.com/** and selecting **DOWNLOAD & SHOP** and **Buy Windows 8**.

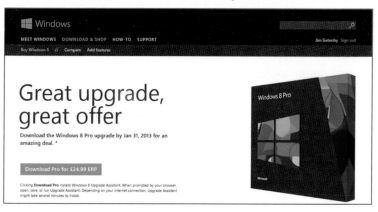

Tap or click the green **Download Pro** button shown above.

- This downloads a program called the Windows 8 Upgrade Assistant. The Assistant checks that your computer can run Windows 8 and also checks for any compatibility issues.

- If Windows 8 can run, proceed to the purchase section. You can now order Windows 8 and a backup CD if you wish. Then enter your name, address and credit card details.

- After completing the order, a receipt is e-mailed to you, together with your Windows 8 *product code*. The product code should be kept safe as it will be needed if you ever reinstall Windows 8.

- Tap or click **Next** to download Windows 8. The time for the download depends on the speed of your Internet connection.

- When the download is complete select **Install now**. There are some other **Install** options but **Install now** is recommended if you are not an advanced user.

- Advanced users may choose the option **Install by creating media**. This enables you to create a copy of the installation software on a DVD or flash drive. This might be needed if you need to carry out a *clean install*, as discussed shortly.

- Windows Setup checks for anything you need to do before the installation starts. This might include closing any running programs which might conflict with the installation.

- When you tap or click **Install** the process begins. The computer will restart several times during the installation.

- After Windows 8 is installed, computers previously running Windows XP and Vista will need to have their apps reinstalled. Data files will not need to be reinstalled.

- Files, apps and settings on computers previously running Windows 7 should all have been transferred to Windows 8 during the installation process.

Installing Windows 8 Pro from a DVD

- In the case of Windows XP and Vista, make sure you have the installation media for the software you wish to reinstall.

- Insert the Windows 8 Pro DVD. Choose either the 32-bit or 64-bit DVD. Use the 32-bit DVD initially if you're not sure.

- Select **Run setup.exe**.

- Enter your 25-character product code. It is located on a small card slotted into the Windows 8 Pro packaging.

- Follow the instructions on the screen.

- Users upgrading from Windows XP and Vista will need to reinstall any previous apps they wish to use in the future.

The Clean Install

So far this section has discussed the installation of Windows 8 Pro on a computer which has an earlier version of Windows still in place on the hard disc drive. The advantage of this method of upgrading to Windows 8 is that your data files (and also your apps in the case of Windows 7) are retained for use with Windows 8. The disadvantage is that an older computer may have accumulated a lot of redundant files on the hard disc drive. This unnecessary debris may slow the computer down.

Some advanced users prefer to carry out a *clean install* rather than inserting Windows 8 over the top of an earlier version such as Windows 7. A future clean install may also be necessary as a last resort if essential files in Windows 8 become corrupted.

The clean install involves *formatting* the hard disc drive. This removes all existing programs and data files. The computer must then be "booted up" from an installation DVD or flash drive and Windows 8 Pro installed. The disadvantage of this method is that any programs and files you want to keep must be backed up onto media such as a DVD or flash drive before the hard disc drive is formatted. The programs and data files you wish to use in the future must then be installed on the new Windows 8 system from their media such as a DVD or flash drive.

The Hard Disc Partition - Dual Boot System

Instead of formatting the whole hard disc drive, if space allows you can create a *partition* on the hard disc which acts like a separate drive. This is formatted and Windows 8 Pro copied to the partition as a clean install. The advantage of this method is that you can keep your old operating system such as Windows 7. As the computer starts up you can choose which version of Windows to run during a session, Windows 7 or Windows 8.

If you are new to computing it is advisable to get expert help to carry out a clean install. Without careful backup procedures it might result in the loss of important data and software.

Software for Windows 8 and Windows 8 Pro

Windows 8 and Windows 8 Pro can run software from the following sources:

- Apps placed as tiles on the Start Screen by default when Windows 8 and Windows 8 Pro are installed.

- Apps downloaded from the Windows Store by the user with tiles automatically placed on the Start Screen.

- Traditional Windows software, e.g. designed for Windows XP or Windows 7. This can be installed from the original media. A tile is placed on the Start Screen.

Apps installed with tiles on the Start Screen by default and apps from the Windows Store were discussed earlier in this book. The next section describes the installing of traditional Windows software on Windows 8 and Windows 8 Pro. For example, you may want to use Windows 8 to run some of your favourite programs designed for Windows XP and Windows 7, such as word processing, spreadsheet, desktop publishing, graphics and photo editing software.

Programs designed for Windows XP, Vista or Windows 7 should be compatible with Windows 8 and Windows 8 Pro. Some of the most popular traditional Windows software includes Microsoft Word and the Microsoft Excel spreadsheet. These are widely used in business all over the world.

Traditional programs written for Windows XP, Vista and Windows 7 will not run on Windows RT in their original form. Special versions of Microsoft Word, Excel, PowerPoint and OneNote have been produced for Windows RT.

Installing Traditional Software (Publisher 2010)

Microsoft Publisher 2010 is part of the Microsoft Office suite of software and can be used for creating all sorts of publications including books such as this one. It is widely used on computers running Windows XP and Windows 7 and can be installed on Windows 8 as described below.

With the Windows 8 Start Screen displayed, insert the Publisher DVD. A message appears in the top right-hand corner of the screen telling you to **Tap to choose what happens with this disc**. Tap or click in the blue area then select **Run SETUP.EXE** from the menu which pops up, as shown on the right. Next you are asked to enter your 25-character Product Key. This is normally found on the packaging for the software, perhaps on a label.

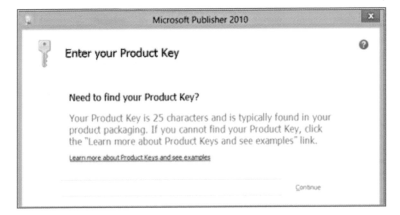

The installation of the software is now automatic and should only take a few minutes, after which you need to restart the computer to complete the process.

Publisher should appear in the All apps screen as shown on the right. Opening the All apps screen is discussed on  page 13. Briefly hold then swipe the app up or down or right click with a mouse to display the following toolbar across the bottom of the screen.

Then tap or click **Pin to Start** shown above to place a tile for Publisher on the Start Screen. The toolbar shown above can also be used to **Uninstall** programs that are no longer required. Displaying the Start Screen and All apps toolbars is also discussed on page 104. Tap the new tile to open Publisher in the traditional Desktop with the Ribbon across the top and the Taskbar along the bottom, as shown below.

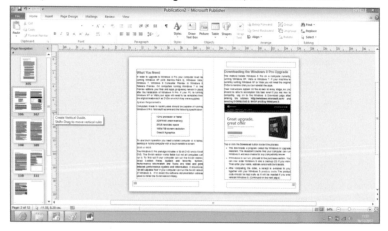

Software for Use with Windows RT

Windows RT runs on tablet computers with the ARM processor. These computers can't run original versions of software designed for operating systems such as Windows XP and Windows 7.

The only sources of software for Windows RT are:

- Apps placed as tiles by default on the Start Screen of a new computer on which Windows RT is pre-installed.

- These include special versions of Microsoft Word, Excel, PowerPoint and OneNote which have been converted to run on Windows RT.

- Apps downloaded from the Windows Store with a tile automatically placed on the Start Screen.

Apps installed as tiles on the Start Screen by default and apps from the Windows Store were discussed earlier in this book. The next section outlines the Office 2013 software which is included with Windows RT. The four apps appear as tiles on the Start Screen of a new RT tablet as shown on the right below. These are Preview editions of Word 2013, Excel 2013, PowerPoint 2013 and OneNote 2013, specially converted to run on Windows RT.

Microsoft Word is probably the world's most popular word processing program, used for producing anything from a simple letter, to a report or thesis or a complete book such as this one.

Microsoft Excel is a popular spreadsheet program, used for automating the calculation of tables of numbers in accounts and scientific work, including the production of graphs and charts.

PowerPoint is used to make presentations to audiences such as clubs, business meetings or family gatherings. Screens include text and photographs and can be presented in a slide show.

OneNote is a program designed to collect all of your information from different sources and organise it into an easily retrievable single system. Information may include typed notes, Web addresses, Web pages, photos and video clips, for example.

When you tap or click the tile for one of the Office 2013 apps such as Word 2013, the program opens in the traditional Windows Desktop, as shown on the right. The toolbar along the bottom has  icons for One Note, PowerPoint, Word and Excel, as shown below.

Along the top of the Word page shown above is the Office Ribbon, with icons for all the word processing tasks such as page layout, formatting text and saving and printing, as shown below.

Glossary of Terms: Windows 8 & RT

App

A program or application designed for a specific purpose such as accounts, a game, playing music or desktop publishing.

ARM Processor

A design of processor used in tablet computers and mobile phones. Its low power consumption increases battery life in mobile devices.

Charms

A set of icons on the right of the screen. Used for settings, searching the computer, returning to the Start Screen, etc.

Control Panel

A feature which provides access to all of the settings on the computer such as security, screen display and personalization.

Desktop

The main screen used on earlier versions of Windows and included in Windows 8 and RT to run certain applications.

Gestures

Finger movements used to control a touchscreen computer.

Lock Screen

The startup screen. May require a password to proceed.

Metro

The original name for the Modern UI.

Modern UI

The user interface in Windows 8 and RT operated by touchscreen or mouse and keyboard, includes Start Screen, Lock Screen, All apps.

Notification

Brief updates on the screen, e.g. informing you of new e-mails, etc.

Operating System

Software such as Windows 8 and RT used to control the overall operation of the computer, irrespective of what apps are running.

Processor

Microchips which execute programs. The processor is often referred to as the "brains" of the computer.

Program

A set of instructions written in a special language or code used to control the computer. Also known as an app or application.

Start Screen

An array of tiles on the screen used to launch apps and Web pages.

Tablet

A hand-held, battery-powered, touchscreen computer such as the Microsoft Surface or Apple iPad.

Tiles

Small rectangular panels on the Start Screen used to launch apps and Web sites. Live tiles display constantly changing information.

Touchscreen

A screen used to control a computer using finger gestures.

Windows 8

The basic version of Windows 8 installed by computer manufacturers.

Windows 8 Pro

The retail version of Windows 8 sold as a download or DVD for users wishing to upgrade, e.g. from Windows XP, Vista or Windows 7.

Windows RT

A version of Windows 8 specially written for ARM tablet computers.

Windows Store

An online collection of thousands of apps. Apps are either free or can be purchased before downloading to Windows 8 or RT.

x86

A processor specification used in the majority of PC computers such as those running Windows XP, Vista or Windows 7.

Index